Navigating the Digital Playground

Navigating the Digital Playground

A Parent's Guide to Raising Tech-Savvy, Balanced Kids

Published in 2023

ISBN: 9789358814699 (PB)
ISBN: 9789358815238 (eBook)

Published by

Mindful Pages
Imprint of Alpha Editions LLC
312 W. 2nd St #1834
Casper, WY 82601, USA

Contents

Introduction

In an era where technology weaves itself seamlessly into the fabric of our lives, the digital playground is where our children often find themselves at play. With each swipe, click, or tap, they embark on adventures, connect with friends, and discover a world that is both awe-inspiring and full of possibilities. Our children are growing up in a digital age, a reality unlike any other generation has experienced before.

As parents, we marvel at their innate ability to navigate touchscreens with ease, yet we grapple with the profound responsibility of shepherding them through this brave new world. The screens that illuminate their faces are windows to information, creativity, and a multitude of experiences. But they can also be portals to potential pitfalls, uncharted territories, and digital dilemmas.

The importance of addressing digital well-being for our children cannot be overstated. We are witnesses to the rapid evolution of technology, and with this evolution comes both unprecedented opportunities and unprecedented challenges. How do we ensure that our children harness the power of technology for their benefit, while simultaneously guarding them against its potential harm?

This is the core question at the heart of "Navigating the Digital Playground: A Parent's Guide to Raising Tech-Savvy, Balanced Kids." In the pages that follow, we embark on a journey together, a journey that seeks to equip you, the parent, with the knowledge, tools, and insights needed to guide your child through this complex digital terrain.

The task before us is not merely about setting screen time limits or installing parental control software; it's about nurturing tech-savvy, balanced individuals who can thrive in a world where technology is an integral part of their existence. It's about fostering open lines of communication so that our children feel safe to share their digital experiences, dilemmas, and dreams. It's about empowering them to make wise choices, develop critical thinking skills, and engage responsibly in the digital realm.

As we delve into the various facets of digital well-being for children, we will explore age-appropriate technology usage, online safety, the art of setting digital boundaries, promoting digital literacy, and striking that delicate balance between screen time and offline activities. We will uncover strategies to address cyberbullying, nurture positive online behavior, and, perhaps most importantly, be role models ourselves in the digital world.

Through practical advice, real-world examples, and expert insights, "Navigating the Digital Playground" aims to be your trusted companion on this ever-evolving journey. Together, we will discover that the digital playground is not a realm to be feared but a landscape to be navigated with care, knowledge, and above all, love.

Welcome to a guide that empowers you to raise tech-savvy, balanced kids who can embrace the digital age with confidence and resilience. Welcome to "Navigating the Digital Playground."

My motivation for writing "Navigating the Digital Playground: A Parent's Guide to Raising Tech-Savvy, Balanced Kids" stems from a deep concern and a genuine passion for the well-being of our children in an increasingly digital world. As a parent myself, I've witnessed firsthand the challenges and dilemmas that come with raising children immersed in technology. I've seen the transformative power of screens, from educational tools that inspire curiosity to potential distractions that hinder development. It became evident that navigating this digital landscape required a roadmap, one that balanced the benefits of technology with its potential risks.

The motivation extends beyond personal experience. In an age where technology evolves at breakneck speed, parents worldwide grapple with similar concerns: How can we ensure our children harness the opportunities technology offers while staying safe and balanced? I believe that by equipping parents with practical knowledge, informed strategies, and a sense of empowerment, we can foster responsible digital citizens who thrive in the digital age.

Furthermore, as a writer for digital well-being, I am driven to bridge the gap between the digital world and parenting. This book is my contribution to this vital conversation. I aspire to empower parents with the tools they need to navigate the digital playground confidently, fostering a generation of tech-savvy, balanced, and resilient children who can flourish in the digital era while preserving the values and lessons that define our human experience. Ultimately, my motivation is to help families embark on this digital journey with knowledge, purpose, and the unwavering belief that they can shape a positive and enriching digital future for their children.

1

Understanding the Digital Landscape: Navigating the Technological Terrain of Childhood

The digital landscape in which our children are growing up is a remarkable, ever-evolving realm that simultaneously captivates and challenges parents and educators alike. In this chapter, we embark on a journey to comprehend the multifaceted world that our young ones are navigating with such ease and enthusiasm.

The Digital Playground: A Digital-First Generation Today's children belong to a digital-first generation, born into a world where smartphones, tablets, and the internet are as ubiquitous as the air they breathe. For them, digital devices and online connectivity are not mere tools; they are extensions of their daily lives, integral to their education, entertainment, and social interactions.

The Pervasiveness of Screens Screens are omnipresent, captivating young minds from the moment they can focus their gaze. Whether it's the colorful allure of educational apps on a tablet, the mesmerizing worlds of video games, or the endless scroll of social media feeds, screens are a constant presence. This pervasive screen culture raises important questions about the quantity and quality of screen time that children are exposed to.

Technology as a Double-Edged Sword The digital landscape offers a double-edged sword of opportunities and challenges. On one hand, it provides access to a vast wealth of information, educational resources, and creative outlets. On the other, it presents potential risks, including exposure to inappropriate content, cyberbullying, and addiction-like behaviors.

The Social Network Phenomenon Children are not only consumers of digital content but active participants in the global social network phenomenon. They engage in online friendships, share personal experiences through photos and videos, and communicate via text, emojis, and memes. The digital realm has become a primary avenue for socializing and identity development.

The Technological Generation Gap Understanding the digital landscape also means acknowledging the generation gap that often exists between children and their parents or caregivers. Many adults did not grow up with the same level of digital immersion, leading to challenges in comprehending the nuances of online interactions and staying updated with the latest technologies.

A Rapidly Evolving Technological Frontier The digital landscape is in a state of constant flux, with new technologies, platforms, and trends emerging regularly. Keeping pace with these changes is a formidable task, especially for parents who may feel overwhelmed by the sheer volume of information and choices available.

In Conclusion The digital landscape our children inhabit is a complex ecosystem that offers both extraordinary opportunities and potential pitfalls. To navigate this terrain effectively, parents must strive to understand its dynamics, embrace its potential, and remain vigilant to protect and guide their children. As we delve deeper into the chapters of this book, we will explore strategies for harnessing the digital world's benefits while mitigating its risks, fostering digital literacy, and nurturing a balanced approach to technology in our children's lives. In doing so, we equip ourselves to be informed and proactive guides in our children's digital journeys.

Benefits and Challenges of Technology for Kids

In today's digital age, technology plays an undeniable role in the lives of children. From smartphones and tablets to educational apps and online learning platforms, technology offers both benefits and challenges in shaping the experiences of young individuals.

Benefits of Technology for Kids:

Educational Opportunities: Technology provides access to a vast array of educational resources. Interactive apps, e-books, and educational websites make learning engaging and accessible, allowing children to explore subjects and concepts beyond traditional classroom settings.

Enhanced Creativity: Digital tools, such as art and music apps, enable children to express their creativity and imagination. They can create digital art, compose music, and even produce their own videos, fostering artistic development.

Global Connectivity: Technology connects children with peers and cultures from around the world. Social media, video calls, and online gaming enable them to build friendships and gain a broader perspective on global issues.

Customized Learning: Adaptive learning platforms can tailor educational content to a child's individual pace and level of understanding, providing a personalized learning experience.

Skill Development: Technology can aid in the development of essential skills, including problem-solving, critical thinking, and digital literacy. These skills are increasingly important in the digital age.

Accessibility: For children with disabilities, technology can be a powerful tool for accessibility. Screen readers, communication apps, and assistive devices open doors to learning and communication.

Challenges of Technology for Kids:

Screen Time Overuse: Excessive screen time can lead to sedentary behavior and physical health issues. It may also interfere with sleep patterns and lead to addiction-like behaviors, such as compulsive gaming or social media use.

Inappropriate Content: The internet's vastness means that children can stumble upon inappropriate or harmful content. This exposure can have negative emotional and psychological effects.

Cyberbullying: Online spaces can become venues for cyberbullying, where children may experience harassment or social exclusion. This can have severe consequences on their mental health and self-esteem.

Privacy Concerns: Children may not fully understand the implications of sharing personal information online. They can inadvertently disclose sensitive data, making them vulnerable to privacy breaches and identity theft.

Digital Addiction: The allure of technology can lead to digital addiction, where children struggle to disengage from screens and prioritize offline activities.

Loss of Real-World Experiences: An overreliance on technology may limit children's engagement in real-world activities, such as outdoor play, face-to-face social interactions, and hobbies.

Tech Generation Gap: Parents and caregivers may struggle to keep up with rapidly evolving technology, leading to communication gaps and difficulties in monitoring and guiding children's digital activities.

Understanding the benefits and challenges of technology for kids is essential for parents, educators, and caregivers. By striking a balance between technology use and offline activities, promoting responsible digital behavior, and staying involved in children's online experiences, adults can help harness the positive aspects of technology while mitigating its potential drawbacks. Ultimately, technology can be a valuable tool when used thoughtfully and responsibly in a child's life.

2

Age-Appropriate Technology: Navigating the Digital World with Your Child

In today's digital age, it's undeniable that technology has become an integral part of our lives, and this includes the lives of our children. From the moment they are born, children are exposed to various forms of technology, from smartphones and tablets to interactive toys and educational apps. However, ensuring that children use age-appropriate technology is a crucial aspect of responsible parenting in the digital era.

What is Age-Appropriate Technology?

Age-appropriate technology refers to digital devices, content, and applications that are specifically designed to meet the developmental needs and abilities of children within a certain age group. This concept recognizes that children of different ages have varying levels of cognitive, physical, and emotional development, and their exposure to technology should align with these developmental stages.

Why Age-Appropriate Technology Matters:

Cognitive Development: Children go through significant cognitive changes as they grow. Age-appropriate technology can offer activities and content that align with their evolving cognitive abilities, from simple cause-and-effect interactions for infants to more complex problem-solving games for older children.

Social and Emotional Growth: Technology can influence a child's social and emotional development. Age-appropriate technology promotes positive social interactions, empathy, and emotional regulation, while inappropriate content can have adverse effects.

Physical Development: Interactive technology should be designed with attention to fine and gross motor skills. Age-appropriate devices and apps should encourage physical activity and coordination, especially for younger children.

Educational Value: Technology can be a powerful educational tool when used appropriately. Age-appropriate content can reinforce classroom learning, stimulate curiosity, and promote a love for exploration and discovery.

Safety and Privacy: Young children may not fully grasp the concepts of online safety and privacy. Age-appropriate technology should include robust parental controls and safety features to protect children from inappropriate content and online risks.

Guidelines for Choosing Age-Appropriate Technology:

Read Reviews and Ratings: Before introducing a new app or device to your child, read reviews and check ratings from reputable sources. This can provide insights into the content and suitability for your child's age group.

Check Age Ratings: Many app stores and content platforms provide age ratings and guidelines. Be sure to review these ratings to ensure the content aligns with your child's age and maturity level.

Try Before You Buy: Whenever possible, test out technology products yourself or with your child. This allows you to assess the content, usability, and educational value.

Engage in Co-Play: Share technology experiences with your child. Co-play not only strengthens the parent-child bond but also allows you to monitor and guide their interactions with technology.

Set Screen Time Limits: Establish reasonable screen time limits for your child based on their age and developmental stage. Ensure that technology doesn't interfere with other important activities, such as sleep, physical play, and homework.

Stay Informed: Keep yourself updated on the latest trends in children's technology and digital parenting. This knowledge will help you make informed decisions about age-appropriate technology.

In a world where technology continually evolves, responsible parenting means striking a balance between embracing the benefits of age-appropriate technology and safeguarding children from potential risks. By selecting digital tools that align with your child's developmental stage and actively engaging with them in their technology experiences, you can help your child navigate the digital world with confidence and responsibility.

Age-Appropriate Tech Use Guidelines: Nurturing Healthy Digital Habits for Children

As parents and caregivers, one of our paramount responsibilities in the digital age is to establish age-appropriate technology use guidelines for our children. These guidelines serve as a compass, helping children navigate the digital landscape while fostering healthy, responsible, and balanced tech habits. Here's an exploration of age-appropriate tech use guidelines tailored to different age groups:

Infants and Toddlers (0-2 years):

> Minimal Screen Time: The American Academy of Pediatrics (AAP) recommends avoiding screen time for children under 18 months, except for video chatting with family. Between 18 and 24 months, limited, high-quality educational content is acceptable if watched with a caregiver to help them understand what they're seeing.

> Focus on Interaction: Prioritize real-world interactions over screens. Engage in face-to-face play, reading, and physical activities to stimulate their cognitive and social development.

> Choose High-Quality Content: If you introduce digital media, opt for age-appropriate, educational content that encourages active engagement rather than passive viewing.

Preschoolers (3-5 years):

> Limited Screen Time: The AAP recommends a maximum of one hour of screen time per day for this age group. Ensure this time includes high-quality, educational content.

> Co-Viewing and Co-Playing: Watch and play with your child when they use screens. Use this as an opportunity for interaction and learning.

> Create Screen-Free Zones: Designate specific areas in your home, such as bedrooms and the dining room, as screen-free zones to encourage healthy boundaries.

Navigating the Digital Playground

School-Age Children (6-12 years):

Set Screen Time Limits: Establish daily or weekly screen time limits based on your family's needs and values. Include both recreational and educational screen time.

Encourage Educational Content: Encourage children to explore educational apps, websites, and games that align with their interests and learning objectives.

Promote Balance: Emphasize the importance of a balanced routine that includes outdoor play, physical activity, reading, and creative pursuits.

Online Safety Education: Teach children about online safety, privacy, and responsible digital citizenship. Explain the potential risks and how to handle them.

Teenagers (13-18 years):

Negotiate Screen Time: Collaborate with your teenager to set reasonable screen time limits that respect their need for independence and self-regulation.

Monitor Content: Keep an open dialogue about the content they consume and engage with online. Encourage critical thinking about the information they encounter.

Balance with Offline Activities: Ensure they balance screen time with face-to-face interactions, extracurricular activities, homework, and chores.

Cyberbullying Awareness: Discuss cyberbullying, online etiquette, and the importance of treating others with respect in digital spaces.

Digital Well-Being: Encourage self-awareness and self-care regarding screen time. Teach them to recognize signs of digital addiction and how to maintain a healthy digital balance.

Set a Good Example: Model responsible tech use and adhere to similar guidelines yourself.

Remember that these guidelines should be flexible and tailored to your child's individual needs, interests, and developmental stage.

Regularly revisit and adjust them as your child matures and technology evolves. The key is to maintain open communication, foster responsible digital citizenship, and ensure technology serves as a valuable tool for learning and entertainment rather than a hindrance to their overall well-being.

Effects of Screen Time on Different Age Groups

Screen time, which includes time spent on digital devices such as smartphones, tablets, computers, and television, can have varying effects on individuals depending on their age group. Here, we'll explore how screen time impacts different age groups, from young children to adults:

1. Infants and Toddlers (0-2 years):

> Positive Effects: Limited and supervised screen time can introduce infants and toddlers to age-appropriate educational content, such as high-quality videos and interactive apps, which may support language development and early learning.

> Negative Effects: Excessive screen time can hinder healthy brain development, as it replaces critical face-to-face interactions and hands-on activities. It may also disrupt sleep patterns when used before bedtime.

2. Preschoolers (3-5 years):

> Positive Effects: Educational programming and interactive apps can contribute to early literacy, numeracy skills, and cognitive development. Screen time can also provide exposure to diverse cultures and ideas.

> Negative Effects: Excessive screen time may lead to delayed social skills development and decreased physical activity, which can contribute to health issues like obesity. It's essential to balance screen time with other activities.

3. School-Age Children (6-12 years):

> Positive Effects: Screen time can offer educational opportunities, including online research, homework assistance, and creative digital projects. It can also serve as a platform for socializing and building digital literacy skills.

Negative Effects: Excessive screen time can lead to poor posture, digital eye strain, and a sedentary lifestyle. It may also contribute to sleep disturbances if not regulated, affecting academic performance.

4. Teenagers (13-18 years):

Positive Effects: Screen time provides essential tools for academic research, communication, and creative expression. It can also be a source of social connection and support.

Negative Effects: Excessive screen time, especially on social media, can contribute to negative self-esteem, depression, and anxiety. It may also interfere with sleep patterns, impacting academic and emotional well-being.

5. Adults:

Positive Effects: For adults, screen time is a necessary part of work, communication, and access to information. It can enhance productivity, facilitate remote work, and provide entertainment and relaxation.

Negative Effects: Prolonged screen time can lead to digital eye strain, sleep disturbances, and sedentary behavior, which can increase the risk of chronic health conditions such as obesity, heart disease, and diabetes.

6. Older Adults (65+ years):

Positive Effects: Screen time can help older adults stay connected with loved ones through video calls and social media. It can also provide access to educational resources and entertainment, reducing feelings of isolation.

Negative Effects: Excessive screen time can contribute to social isolation if it replaces in-person interactions. It may also lead to physical inactivity if older adults spend prolonged periods sitting in front of screens.

In all age groups, the key to a healthy relationship with screens is moderation, balance, and mindful usage. Parents and caregivers should set appropriate screen time limits for children, and adults should be aware of their own screen time habits. Regular breaks, physical activity, and offline interactions are essential for mitigating the negative effects of screen time on physical and mental health. Additionally, staying informed about age-appropriate content and ensuring that screen time serves educational and recreational purposes can help maximize its benefits.

Introducing Technology to Young Children: Creative Approaches

Introducing technology to young children can be a valuable educational experience when done mindfully and creatively. Here are some recommendations and creative ways to do so:

1. Interactive Learning Apps and Games:

> Situation: You want to introduce your preschooler to educational apps.

> Example: Choose apps that focus on early literacy, numeracy, and problem-solving. Play these apps together, offering guidance and encouragement. For instance, explore apps that teach letter recognition through interactive alphabet games, or use math apps that make learning numbers fun with engaging visuals and challenges.

2. Virtual Field Trips:

> Situation: You're looking for ways to make learning about the world engaging.

> Example: Take your child on virtual field trips using educational websites and videos. Explore a virtual zoo, museum, or historical site. Discuss what you see together, ask questions, and encourage curiosity. Follow up with related activities like drawing or crafting based on what you've learned.

3. Creative Content Creation:

> Situation: You want to encourage your child's creativity and storytelling skills.

> Example: Use digital devices to inspire creativity. Encourage your child to create digital stories, drawings, or even short videos. You can use simple drawing apps for

digital art projects or record them telling a story. This fosters their imagination and digital literacy.

4. Educational YouTube Channels:

Situation: You're seeking a resource for age-appropriate, educational content.

Example: Find YouTube channels specifically designed for children's education. For instance, there are channels that focus on science experiments, art projects, or animated storytelling. Watch these videos together, and afterward, engage in discussions or hands-on activities related to what you've seen.

5. Nature Exploration with Apps:

Situation: You want to combine technology with outdoor exploration.

Example: Use nature exploration apps that help your child identify plants, insects, or bird species during outdoor walks. These apps often include interactive features like taking photos and recording observations, making nature walks more engaging and educational.

6. Family Virtual Book Club:

Situation: You'd like to encourage a love of reading.

Example: Start a family virtual book club where you read age-appropriate e-books together. Use tablets or e-readers to access digital books. Discuss the story, characters, and themes as a family. You can even take turns reading aloud.

7. Cooking Adventures with Recipes Apps:

Situation: You want to involve your child in the kitchen.

Example: Find a cooking or recipe app suitable for children. Cook together, following the digital recipe step by step. This not only teaches cooking skills but also reinforces math and reading abilities as your child follows instructions.

8. Digital Puzzles and Brain Games:

> Situation: You want to promote problem-solving and critical thinking.

> Example: Explore digital puzzle games, riddles, and brain teasers. These apps challenge children's cognitive skills in a fun way. You can work together to solve puzzles or take turns.

9. Virtual Music Lessons:

> Situation: You'd like to introduce music and rhythm.

> Example: Consider virtual music lessons or apps that teach children how to play simple instruments like a keyboard or guitar. Learning music through interactive apps can be engaging and provide a foundation for future musical interests.

Remember that the key to introducing technology to young children is to be actively involved in their digital experiences. Use technology as a tool for learning and exploration, and always maintain open communication with your child about their screen time. By incorporating technology creatively and purposefully into their routine, you can help them develop digital literacy and foster a love for learning.

3
Online Safety and Privacy

In our increasingly connected world, the internet offers immense opportunities for communication, learning, entertainment, and more. However, as we navigate the digital landscape, it's crucial to prioritize online safety and privacy. This comprehensive guide explores the importance of online safety and privacy, offering strategies and best practices to protect yourself and your information in the digital realm.

Understanding the Digital Landscape

Before delving into online safety and privacy measures, it's essential to comprehend the digital landscape we inhabit. The internet is a vast and dynamic space where information flows freely, but it also harbors risks and threats. Here are some key aspects to consider:

Digital Footprint: Every online action, from social media posts to online purchases, contributes to your digital footprint. This trail of data can be tracked, stored, and potentially misused by various entities.

Cyberthreats: The internet is home to cyberthreats, including hackers, phishing scams, malware, and identity theft. These threats can target individuals, organizations, and even governments.

Privacy Concerns: The digital world often blurs the line between public and private information. Many online services and platforms collect and monetize user data, raising concerns about data privacy and surveillance.

Social Engineering: Cybercriminals employ social engineering tactics to manipulate individuals into divulging sensitive information. This can include impersonation, emotional manipulation, or exploiting trust.

Online Behavior: Your online behavior and interactions can impact your safety and reputation. What you share, how you communicate, and the communities you engage with all play a role.

Why Online Safety and Privacy Matter

Online safety and privacy are paramount for several compelling reasons:

Protection from Cyberthreats: Maintaining strong online security safeguards your personal information, finances, and digital identity from malicious actors.

Preservation of Reputation: Your online behavior and digital footprint can affect your personal and professional reputation. Responsible online conduct is crucial.

Prevention of Identity Theft: Safeguarding personal information, such as social security numbers and financial details, is essential to prevent identity theft.

Data Privacy: Protecting your data ensures that it isn't misused, sold, or accessed without your consent.

Emotional Well-being: Online safety extends to emotional well-being, shielding individuals from cyberbullying, harassment, and online abuse.

Online Safety Measures

To enhance your online safety, consider implementing the following measures:

Strong, Unique Passwords: Use complex, unique passwords for each online account. Consider a password manager to help you generate and store passwords securely.

Two-Factor Authentication (2FA): Enable 2FA whenever possible. It adds an extra layer of security by requiring a second form of verification, such as a code sent to your phone.

Regular Software Updates: Keep your operating system, antivirus software, and applications up to date to patch vulnerabilities that hackers could exploit.

Vigilance Against Phishing: Be cautious of unsolicited emails, messages, and links. Verify the sender's identity and avoid clicking on suspicious links or downloading attachments from unknown sources.

Secure Wi-Fi Connections: Use strong, encrypted Wi-Fi passwords at home, and avoid public Wi-Fi for sensitive transactions like online banking.

Privacy Settings: Review and adjust privacy settings on social media platforms and other online services to control what information you share and who can see it.

Data Encryption: Use encrypted messaging apps and websites (look for "https://" in URLs) to protect the confidentiality of your communications.

Regular Backups: Back up your important data regularly to prevent loss in case of data breaches or hardware failures.

Digital Literacy: Educate yourself about common online threats, scams, and best practices for safe internet usage. Share this knowledge with family members, especially children.

Online Privacy Measures

In addition to online safety, protecting your privacy in the digital age is crucial:

Limit Sharing of Personal Information: Only provide necessary personal information when filling out online forms or creating accounts. Avoid sharing sensitive details unless absolutely required.

Review Privacy Policies: Familiarize yourself with the privacy policies of websites and apps you use. Understand how your data is collected, stored, and shared.

Use Privacy Tools: Consider using virtual private networks (VPNs) to mask your IP address and enhance online anonymity. Browser extensions like ad blockers and privacy-focused search engines can also help.

Location and GPS: Disable location services for apps that don't require it. Regularly review the apps that have access to your location information.

Social Media Awareness: Be mindful of what you share on social media. Avoid posting sensitive personal information such as your address, phone number, or financial details.

Email Encryption: Use encrypted email services or encryption plugins for sensitive email communications.

Protecting Children Online

Online safety and privacy are especially critical for children who are growing up in the digital age. Parents and caregivers should take proactive measures to protect their children online:

Educate and Communicate: Teach children about online safety, privacy, and responsible digital behavior. Encourage open communication so they feel comfortable reporting any concerning online experiences.

Parental Controls: Use parental control software and settings to restrict access to age-inappropriate content and monitor screen time.

Online Etiquette: Teach children about good online etiquette, including the importance of kindness, respect, and responsible communication.

Safe Browsing: Set safe search filters on search engines and enable restricted mode on video-sharing platforms to filter out inappropriate content.

Privacy Settings: Help children configure privacy settings on their devices and social media accounts to limit exposure to strangers.

Supervision: Monitor your child's online activities, especially when they are young, to ensure their safety

Strategies for Protecting Children's Privacy Online

Protecting children's privacy online is crucial in today's digital world. Here are effective strategies to safeguard your child's personal information and ensure a safe online experience:

Educate Your Child:

> Start with age-appropriate conversations about online privacy. Explain why it's essential to keep personal information private and discuss potential risks.

> Emphasize the importance of not sharing sensitive details like full names, addresses, phone numbers, and school names online.

Set Clear Boundaries:

> Establish rules and guidelines for your child's online activities. Discuss when and where they can use devices, how much screen time is allowed, and which websites or apps are off-limits.

> Make sure your child understands these rules and the consequences of not following them.

Use Parental Control Software:

> Implement parental control software or apps that allow you to monitor and manage your child's online activities. These tools often include features like content filtering, screen time limits, and activity tracking.

> Familiarize yourself with the settings and features of the parental control software to customize it according to your child's age and needs.

Protect Personal Devices:

> Secure personal devices, such as smartphones and tablets, with strong passwords or PINs to prevent unauthorized access.

> Activate device lock features like fingerprint or facial recognition where available.

Review App Permissions:

> Before downloading or allowing your child to use a new app or game, review the permissions it requests. Be cautious of apps that ask for excessive personal information or access to device features that aren't relevant to their function.

> Opt for apps with good privacy practices and positive reviews from reputable sources.

Use Child-Friendly Platforms:

> Choose child-friendly online platforms and services designed specifically for young users. These often have enhanced privacy protections and age-appropriate content.

> Be cautious of platforms that allow users to interact with strangers or have minimal moderation.

Teach Safe Social Media Use:

> If your child is old enough to use social media, teach them about privacy settings and the importance of only accepting friend or follower requests from people they know in real life.

> Encourage them to report any inappropriate or suspicious activity to you or the platform administrators.

Monitor Online Activity:

> Keep an eye on your child's online activity without invading their privacy. Periodically review their online accounts and messages to ensure their safety.

> Maintain open communication so your child feels comfortable discussing their online experiences with you.

Promote Safe Online Gaming:

> If your child enjoys online gaming, set guidelines for in-game interactions and chat features. Ensure

they understand the importance of not sharing personal information with other players.

Consider using gaming platforms that offer parental controls and safety features.

Regularly Update Devices and Apps:

Keep your child's devices and apps up to date with the latest security patches and updates. Outdated software can be vulnerable to security risks.

Configure automatic updates when possible to ensure timely protection.

Use Encrypted Communication Tools:

Encourage your child to use encrypted messaging apps when communicating with friends or family members. These apps provide an extra layer of security for their conversations.

Model Responsible Online Behavior:

Children learn by example, so demonstrate responsible online behavior. Show them how to protect their privacy and respect others' privacy online.

Avoid oversharing personal information on social media or in public forums.

Report Suspicious Activity:

Teach your child how to recognize and report suspicious or inappropriate content, messages, or interactions. Many online platforms have reporting mechanisms for such situations.

Regularly Reinforce Privacy Education:

Privacy education is an ongoing process. Regularly revisit and reinforce online safety and privacy lessons as your child grows and encounters new digital experiences.

Stay Informed:

- Keep yourself informed about the latest online privacy and security trends and threats. This knowledge will help you adapt your strategies to evolving risks.

By implementing these strategies and fostering open communication, you can protect your child's privacy online while teaching them essential skills for responsible digital citizenship. Remember that age-appropriate discussions and gradual independence in online activities are essential for their growth and safety in the digital world.

Tips for Educating Kids About Online Dangers

Educating kids about online dangers is crucial to help them navigate the digital world safely. Here are tips to effectively teach them about potential online risks and how to protect themselves:

Start Early:

Begin age-appropriate discussions about online safety and dangers as soon as your child starts using digital devices. Lay a foundation for responsible online behavior from the start.

Be Open and Approachable:

Create an environment where your child feels comfortable discussing their online experiences, concerns, or questions without fear of punishment or judgment.

Use Real-Life Examples:

Share real-world examples of online dangers and their consequences. Use news stories, case studies, or incidents involving people they can relate to, if possible.

Discuss Privacy:

Teach your child the concept of personal information and the importance of keeping it private. Explain that personal information includes their name, address, phone number, school, and even photos that reveal their location.

Online Persona vs. Real Identity:

Help your child understand the difference between their online persona and their real identity. Emphasize that not everyone online is who they claim to be.

Stranger Danger:

Explain that just as they should be cautious of strangers in the physical world, they should be equally cautious of strangers online. Encourage them to avoid sharing personal information with people they don't know in real life.

Cyberbullying Awareness:

Discuss the harmful effects of cyberbullying and the importance of treating others with kindness and respect online. Teach your child how to recognize and respond to cyberbullying situations.

Online Etiquette:

Teach good online etiquette, including using appropriate language, refraining from sharing hurtful content, and being mindful of others' feelings.

Recognizing Scams and Hoaxes:

Explain that not everything online is trustworthy. Teach your child to recognize common online scams, phishing attempts, and hoaxes.

Setting Privacy Controls:

Show your child how to set privacy controls on social media platforms, online games, and other apps they use. Help them understand the importance of limiting who can see their content.

Password Safety:

> Teach your child the importance of strong, unique passwords. Encourage them to create passwords that are hard to guess and never share them with anyone except trusted adults.

Safe Online Shopping:

> Explain the risks of online shopping and the importance of using secure websites for purchases. Emphasize that they should only shop online with your permission and assistance.

Reporting Concerns:

> Teach your child how to report any uncomfortable or suspicious online interactions to you or a trusted adult. Familiarize them with reporting mechanisms on websites and apps they use.

Digital Footprint:

> Help your child understand that their online actions leave a digital footprint. Discuss how the content they post can impact their future, including college and job opportunities.

Critical Thinking:

> Encourage critical thinking skills by asking questions like, "Is this information reliable?" or "Could this be a scam?" Teach them to fact-check information and question what they encounter online.

Use Educational Resources:

> Utilize age-appropriate online safety resources and educational games or videos designed to teach kids about online dangers and responsible internet use.

Lead by Example:

> Model responsible online behavior and adhere to the same rules and guidelines you set for your child. Children often learn best through observation.

Revisit and Reinforce:

> Regularly revisit online safety discussions and reinforce lessons as your child's digital experiences evolve. Adjust your guidance to match their age and increasing independence online.

By taking a proactive and ongoing approach to educating your child about online dangers, you empower them to make informed and responsible choices in the digital world, ultimately ensuring their safety and well-being online.

Setting Digital Boundaries

In today's hyperconnected world, setting digital boundaries has become increasingly significant for individuals, families, and communities. These boundaries help manage the use of technology and the internet, promoting well-being, privacy, and healthy relationships. Here's a deeper exploration of the importance of setting digital boundaries:

1. Protecting Privacy:

> Digital boundaries safeguard personal information and privacy. They help individuals control what they share online, limiting the risk of identity theft, cyberbullying, or invasive data collection by companies and malicious actors.

2. Managing Screen Time:

> Establishing boundaries around screen time is essential, especially for children and teens. It prevents excessive device use, which can lead to physical health problems, sleep disturbances, and addiction-like behaviors.

3. Promoting Healthy Relationships:

> Digital boundaries foster healthier relationships by preventing technology from interfering with face-to-face interactions. Setting limits on device usage during family meals, gatherings, and quality time helps strengthen bonds and communication.

4. Maintaining Focus and Productivity:

> Boundaries in the workplace and educational settings help individuals maintain focus and productivity. By limiting distractions from personal devices and social media during work or study hours, individuals can achieve better outcomes.

5. Preventing Cyberbullying:

For children and teenagers, setting digital boundaries can protect them from cyberbullying and online harassment. Limiting exposure to potential bullies or negative online spaces can mitigate the emotional and psychological impact of such experiences.

6. Reducing Digital Exhaustion:

Digital boundaries help reduce digital exhaustion or "screen fatigue." Constant connectivity and information overload can lead to stress and burnout, but clear boundaries on when and how technology is used can alleviate these issues.

7. Ensuring Digital Well-Being:

Setting boundaries contributes to overall digital well-being. It encourages individuals to take breaks, practice mindfulness, and engage in offline activities that promote physical and mental health.

8. Protecting Children and Adolescents:

Parents and caregivers play a crucial role in setting digital boundaries for their children. These boundaries protect young users from age-inappropriate content, online predators, and the negative effects of excessive screen time.

9. Enhancing Self-Control:

Digital boundaries support self-control and discipline. They teach individuals to manage their impulses and make intentional choices regarding technology use, fostering greater autonomy and responsibility.

10. Encouraging Thoughtful Tech Use: - Boundaries encourage thoughtful tech use by prompting individuals to consider the purpose and value of their online activities. This can lead to more intentional and fulfilling digital experiences.

11. Mitigating Digital Addiction: - Excessive use of technology can lead to digital addiction, characterized by a compulsive need to use devices or apps. Setting boundaries is a proactive step in preventing or addressing such addictions.

12. Preserving Family Time: - For families, digital boundaries preserve quality family time. By designating tech-free hours or zones, families can strengthen their relationships and create lasting memories.

13. Cultivating Digital Literacy: - Setting digital boundaries can facilitate discussions about digital literacy and responsible online behavior. It encourages individuals to think critically about the content they encounter and share.

To summarise, setting digital boundaries is not about rejecting technology but about using it mindfully and purposefully. It empowers individuals to maintain control over their digital lives, protect their well-being, and make informed choices. Whether in personal relationships, education, or the workplace, establishing these boundaries is essential for fostering a healthy, balanced, and safe digital environment.

Practical Advice on Establishing Screen Time Limits

Setting screen time limits is essential for maintaining a healthy balance between technology use and other aspects of life, such as family time, physical activity, and sleep. Here are practical tips to help you establish and enforce screen time limits effectively:

Understand Age-Appropriate Guidelines:

> Familiarize yourself with recommended screen time guidelines for different age groups. These guidelines, often provided by reputable organizations like the American Academy of Pediatrics, can serve as a starting point for setting limits.

Set Clear and Consistent Rules:

> Establish clear and consistent rules regarding when and how screens can be used. Make sure everyone in the household understands and agrees to these rules.

Use Screen Time Apps and Features:

> Many devices and operating systems offer built-in parental control features. Use these tools to set

daily or weekly screen time limits for each user or device.

Create a Family Media Plan:

Develop a family media plan that outlines screen time rules and expectations. Involve your children in the planning process, making them aware of the guidelines.

Designate Screen-Free Zones and Times:

Designate certain areas of your home as screen-free zones, such as the dining room and bedrooms. Also, establish screen-free times, such as during meals or before bedtime.

Lead by Example:

Model responsible screen time behavior. Children are more likely to follow rules when they see adults adhering to them. Avoid excessive screen use, especially during designated family time.

Create a Screen Time Schedule:

Develop a daily or weekly schedule that includes allocated screen time for different purposes, such as homework, entertainment, and educational activities. Stick to this schedule as closely as possible.

Use Screen Time as a Reward:

Frame screen time as a reward for completing chores, homework, or other responsibilities. This reinforces the idea that screens are a privilege to be earned.

Prioritize Quality Content:

Encourage your children to prioritize quality content and educational apps during their screen time. Help them select age-appropriate, educational, and engaging material.

Discuss Screen Time Limits Regularly:

> Have open and ongoing discussions about screen time limits with your children. Explain the reasons behind the limits and the benefits of balancing screen time with other activities.

Set Time Alarms or Reminders:

> Use timers, alarms, or reminders to signal the end of screen time sessions. This provides a clear signal that it's time to transition to other activities.

Offer Alternatives:

> Provide alternative activities for children to engage in when screen time ends. Encourage physical activities, reading, hobbies, or family interactions.

Monitor and Review:

> Regularly monitor your child's screen time to ensure compliance with the established limits. Periodically review and adjust these limits as your child's needs and interests change.

Encourage Screen-Free Days:

> Designate certain days as screen-free days or weekends. Use these opportunities to engage in outdoor activities, family outings, or creative pursuits.

Be Flexible but Consistent:

> While it's important to be flexible to accommodate different circumstances, such as school projects or special occasions, consistency in enforcing screen time limits is key to their effectiveness.

Discuss Online Safety:

> Combine discussions about screen time limits with conversations about online safety and responsible digital behavior. Teach your children to be critical thinkers and responsible digital citizens.

Seek Input and Feedback:

> Involve your children in the process of setting and adjusting screen time limits. Encourage them to share their thoughts, concerns, and feedback about the rules.

Celebrate Success:

> Recognize and celebrate your child's adherence to screen time limits and responsible tech use. Positive reinforcement can reinforce good habits.

Remember that the goal of setting screen time limits is not to eliminate screen use entirely but to strike a balance that promotes well-rounded development, physical health, and healthy relationships with technology. Adapt the guidelines to your family's needs, and be patient and consistent as you work together to establish healthy screen time habits.

Enforcing rules consistently, especially when it comes to screen time limits and other digital boundaries, is essential for their effectiveness. Here are methods and strategies to help you enforce rules consistently:

Establish Clear Expectations:

> Ensure that everyone in the family understands the rules and expectations. Use simple and age-appropriate language to explain the guidelines.

Create a Written Family Agreement:

> Draft a family agreement that outlines the rules and consequences for violating them. Have all family members sign it to signify their commitment to following the rules.

Lead by Example:

> Demonstrate responsible behavior by following the rules yourself. Children are more likely to comply when they see adults adhering to the same guidelines.

Consistent Communication:

> Maintain open and consistent communication about the rules and their importance. Discuss the reasons behind the rules and how they contribute to the family's well-being.

Set Reminders and Alarms:

> Use timers, alarms, or digital reminders to signal the beginning and end of screen time sessions. These cues help create a structured routine.

Use Parental Control Tools:

> Utilize parental control apps and features available on devices and platforms to automate and enforce screen time limits. These tools can restrict access to devices and apps once the allotted time is up.

Implement Logical Consequences:

> Establish logical consequences for rule violations. For example, if a child exceeds their screen time limit, the consequence may be a reduction in their next screen time session.

Reward Positive Behavior:

> Implement a reward system for adhering to the rules. Offer incentives for consistently following screen time limits, such as additional privileges or special treats.

Consistent Routine:

> Develop a consistent daily or weekly routine that includes designated times for screen use, chores, homework, and other activities. Stick to this routine as closely as possible.

Be Firm but Fair:

> Maintain a firm stance when enforcing rules, but also be fair and understanding. Listen to your child's concerns or requests for exceptions and make adjustments when appropriate.

Avoid Negotiating During Enforcement:

> While it's important to listen to your child's concerns, avoid negotiating the rules in the midst of rule enforcement. Make adjustments during designated review periods.

Review and Adjust Rules:

> Periodically review and adjust the rules as your child grows and their needs change. Involve your child in these discussions to make them feel part of the decision-making process.

Consistency Across Caregivers:

> Ensure that all caregivers or family members are on the same page when it comes to enforcing rules. Consistency among adults is crucial for children's understanding and compliance.

Document Violations:

> Keep a record of rule violations and consequences. This documentation can help track patterns of behavior and serve as a reference during discussions with your child.

Use Natural Consequences:

> Whenever possible, let natural consequences teach valuable lessons. For example, if a child neglects their chores due to excessive screen time, they may run out of clean clothes.

Offer Second Chances:

> Give your child opportunities to correct their behavior. If they violate a rule, offer a second chance to follow the rule before applying consequences.

Stay Calm and Avoid Power Struggles:

> Maintain a calm and composed demeanor when enforcing rules. Avoid power struggles by focusing

on the behavior and consequences rather than engaging in arguments.

Reinforce Positive Behavior:

Consistently praise and reinforce positive behavior when your child follows the rules. Positive reinforcement encourages them to continue making responsible choices.

Remember that enforcing rules consistently requires patience, commitment, and flexibility. While it may be challenging at times, a consistent approach to rule enforcement ultimately promotes a sense of structure, responsibility, and respect within the family.

Promoting Digital Literacy

In today's fast-paced, interconnected world, digital literacy is not just a valuable skill; it's a necessity. It's the key that unlocks the vast treasure chest of knowledge, creativity, and opportunity available on the digital landscape. However, teaching digital literacy need not be a dry or daunting task. In fact, it can be a thrilling adventure, akin to discovering a hidden world full of wonders and mysteries.

Digital Literacy: The Modern-Day Superpower

Imagine digital literacy as a superpower—an ability to navigate, decipher, and harness the immense power of the digital world. Just like your favorite superheroes, you can embark on an exciting journey to develop and refine this superpower. Here's how you can make this journey both fascinating and engaging:

1. Embrace the Digital Universe:

>Start by introducing the digital world as an exciting universe filled with limitless possibilities. Explain that just like explorers chart uncharted territories, digital literacy empowers them to explore the vastness of the internet safely.

2. The Hero's Quest:

>Frame digital literacy as a hero's quest. Encourage your learners to see themselves as heroes embarking on an adventure to conquer challenges, solve digital mysteries, and acquire valuable skills.

3. The Code of the Digital Knights:

>Introduce the concept of the "Code of the Digital Knights," a set of principles and guidelines for responsible and ethical online behavior. Knights are honorable protectors of the digital realm, and each learner can become one.

4. The Digital Treasure Hunt:

Turn the search for reliable information into an exhilarating treasure hunt. Teach learners how to evaluate websites, fact-check information, and uncover hidden gems amidst a sea of digital noise.

5. Unmasking Cyber Villains:

Explore the concept of cyber villains—online threats like phishing scams, malware, and cyberbullies. Teach learners how to recognize these villains and defend against them, turning them into allies rather than adversaries.

6. Creative Storytelling:

Encourage creative storytelling through digital media. Show learners how to use multimedia tools to tell compelling stories, express their ideas, and make an impact on the digital stage.

7. The Art of Digital Diplomacy:

Highlight the importance of digital diplomacy, or the art of engaging respectfully and productively with others online. Teach the art of constructive digital discussions and debates.

8. Code as a Superpower:

Introduce the world of coding as a superpower that lets learners create their digital worlds. Learning to code empowers them to become digital architects, designing solutions to real-world problems.

9. Digital Detective:

Challenge learners to become digital detectives. Teach them to investigate digital mysteries, such as online hoaxes, and uncover the truth using critical thinking and research skills.

10. Cybersecurity Guardians: - Instill a sense of responsibility by introducing learners to the role of cybersecurity guardians. They can learn how to protect their personal information, devices, and networks from digital threats.

11. The Digital Art Gallery: - Showcase the creative side of digital literacy by curating a "Digital Art Gallery" where learners can exhibit

their digital creations, whether it's graphic design, animations, or multimedia projects.

12. Virtual Reality Expeditions: - Take learners on virtual reality (VR) expeditions to explore different aspects of the digital world. Visit the inner workings of a computer, journey through the history of the internet, or even venture into the realm of augmented reality.

13. Real-World Applications: - Demonstrate how digital literacy skills are not confined to the digital world alone. Highlight real-world applications, such as using digital tools for community projects, research, or entrepreneurial endeavors.

14. The Power of Collaboration: - Emphasize the power of collaboration in the digital age. Show learners how to connect, communicate, and collaborate with peers worldwide to tackle global challenges.

15. Digital Ethics Dilemmas: - Explore digital ethics dilemmas with thought-provoking scenarios. Encourage learners to debate ethical questions and develop their own code of digital ethics.

16. Gamify Learning: - Turn digital literacy lessons into interactive games and quests. Gamification can make learning engaging and memorable.

17. The Digital Time Machine: - Create a "Digital Time Machine" where learners can explore the evolution of technology, from ancient computing devices to cutting-edge innovations like artificial intelligence.

18. Celebrate Digital Heroes: - Highlight the stories of digital heroes who have made a positive impact on the world through their digital skills and innovations. Encourage learners to aspire to become digital heroes themselves.

By presenting digital literacy as an exciting journey filled with discovery, challenges, and creative opportunities, you can inspire learners to embrace this modern superpower. In the process, they'll not only develop essential digital skills but also become responsible, ethical, and empowered digital citizens ready to make their mark on the digital world

Emphasizing the Importance of Digital Literacy

In today's digitally-driven world, digital literacy isn't just a valuable skill—it's an essential one. It's the key that unlocks the doors to education, career opportunities, communication, and participation in modern society. Emphasizing the importance of digital literacy is crucial for individuals, communities, and nations. Let's explore why it's such a vital skill:

1. Access to Information: Digital literacy grants individuals access to an unprecedented wealth of information on the internet. It empowers them to seek knowledge, stay informed about current events, and pursue lifelong learning.

2. Educational Empowerment: In the digital age, education has gone beyond textbooks and classrooms. Digital literacy equips students with the ability to research, collaborate, and access educational resources online, enhancing their academic success.

3. Career Readiness: The job market is increasingly competitive, and digital literacy is a core competency for nearly every profession. It's essential for tasks like job searching, resume building, online networking, and remote work.

4. Critical Thinking Skills: Digital literacy fosters critical thinking and problem-solving abilities. It enables individuals to evaluate information critically, discern credible sources from misinformation, and make informed decisions.

5. Communication and Collaboration: Effective communication and collaboration are integral to success in the digital world. Digital literacy helps individuals navigate social media, email, video conferencing, and other communication tools effectively.

6. Financial Literacy: Digital literacy extends to financial literacy, enabling individuals to manage their finances online, make secure digital transactions, and protect themselves from online scams and fraud.

7. Civic Engagement: Informed citizens are the cornerstone of a thriving democracy. Digital literacy enables individuals to engage in civic activities, access government services, and participate in online debates and discussions.

8. Global Citizenship: Digital literacy breaks down geographical barriers, connecting individuals to a global community. It fosters cultural awareness, international collaboration, and a sense of global citizenship.

9. Creative Expression:Digital literacy empowers individuals to express their creativity through digital media, whether it's through art, music, filmmaking, coding, or other forms of digital expression.

10. Entrepreneurship and Innovation: Digital literacy is a catalyst for entrepreneurship and innovation. It equips individuals with the skills to start online businesses, develop digital products, and drive technological advancements.

11. Adaptability and Lifelong Learning: The digital landscape is continually evolving. Digital literacy instills adaptability and a commitment to lifelong learning, ensuring that individuals can keep pace with technological advancements.

12. Social Inclusion: Digital literacy plays a crucial role in social inclusion. It bridges the digital divide, ensuring that marginalized communities have equal access to opportunities and resources.

13. Problem Solving in Complex Issues:Many of the world's most pressing challenges, such as climate change and public health crises, require digital literacy for data analysis, modeling, and collaborative problem-solving.

14. Empowerment and Self-Efficacy: Digital literacy empowers individuals to take control of their digital lives. It fosters a sense of self-efficacy, enabling individuals to navigate technology confidently.

15. Cybersecurity and Digital Safety: In an age of cyber threats, digital literacy is essential for protecting personal information, privacy, and online safety. It teaches individuals how to identify and defend against digital risks.

16. Preservation of Cultural Heritage: Digital literacy aids in the preservation of cultural heritage by enabling the digitization and preservation of historical records, artifacts, and traditions.

17. Innovation in Education: Digital literacy transforms education by enabling innovative teaching methods, personalized learning experiences, and the use of educational technology tools.

18. Social and Economic Development: Nations that prioritize digital literacy see social and economic development. It enhances the workforce's skills, attracts investment, and promotes entrepreneurship.

To sum up, digital literacy is not merely a skill; it's a gateway to a world of opportunities, empowerment, and progress. Emphasizing its importance is not just a matter of personal development but a societal imperative. By equipping individuals with digital literacy skills, we enable them to thrive in the digital age and contribute to the betterment of their communities and the world at large.

Teaching Critical Thinking Skills to Kids

Critical thinking skills are essential for children to become independent, problem-solving, and informed individuals. These skills empower them to analyze information, make reasoned decisions, and navigate the complexities of the world. Here are effective ways to teach critical thinking skills to kids:

Ask Open-Ended Questions: Encourage curiosity and critical thinking by asking open-ended questions that require more than a simple "yes" or "no" answer. Questions like "Why do you think that?" or "What might happen if...?" promote deeper thought.

Promote Problem Solving: Provide opportunities for children to solve real-life problems. These can be as simple as figuring out how to stack blocks or more complex challenges as they grow. Encourage them to brainstorm solutions and evaluate their effectiveness.

Read Actively Together: While reading books together, engage in active discussions about the story, characters, and plot. Ask children to predict what might happen next or how a character might feel in a particular situation.

Encourage Diverse Perspectives: Teach children that there can be multiple valid perspectives on an issue. Discuss topics from various angles, encouraging them to consider different viewpoints and empathize with others.

Engage in Socratic Questioning: Introduce Socratic questioning, a method that encourages critical thinking through a series of questions. Begin with a basic question, then ask follow-up questions that delve deeper into the topic.

Teach Information Evaluation: Help children learn how to assess the reliability of information they encounter. Discuss credible sources, fact-checking, and the importance of verifying information before accepting it as true.

Play Brain-Boosting Games: Engage in games and activities that stimulate critical thinking. Games like chess, Sudoku, brainteasers, and logic puzzles help children develop problem-solving and analytical skills.

Explore "What If" Scenarios: Encourage imaginative thinking by exploring "What if" scenarios. Ask questions like "What if you could fly?" or "What if you could talk to animals?" This fosters creativity and critical thinking.

Discuss Cause and Effect: Help children understand cause-and-effect relationships in everyday situations. Discuss the consequences of their actions and decisions, fostering an awareness of how choices impact outcomes.

Expose Them to Diverse Literature: Read books and stories that expose children to different cultures, historical events, and social issues. This broadens their perspective and encourages critical thinking about the world around them.

Encourage Reflection: Encourage children to reflect on their experiences, thoughts, and feelings. Journaling or regular discussions about their day can help them develop self-awareness and critical reflection skills.

Debate and Discussion: Engage in age-appropriate debates or discussions about various topics. Encourage children to present their opinions with supporting arguments and listen to others' viewpoints respectfully.

Model Critical Thinking: Model critical thinking by talking through your decision-making processes. Explain how you assess information, solve problems, and make choices based on evidence and reasoning.

Encourage Curiosity: Nurture children's innate curiosity by supporting their interests and encouraging exploration. When they ask questions, help them find answers through research and experimentation.

Use Real-Life Examples: Use real-life situations and news stories to discuss critical thinking concepts. Analyze current events together, highlighting critical thinking skills such as skepticism and evidence evaluation.

Provide a Safe Environment: Create a safe space where children feel comfortable expressing their thoughts, even if they differ from yours. Encourage them to ask questions without fear of judgment.

Celebrate Mistakes:Emphasize that making mistakes is a natural part of learning. Encourage a growth mindset where children view errors as opportunities for improvement and learning.

Encourage Independence: Gradually encourage children to make decisions and solve problems independently, offering guidance and support as needed. This fosters a sense of autonomy and self-reliance.

By incorporating these strategies into everyday activities and conversations, you can help children develop and strengthen their critical thinking skills. These skills will serve them well throughout their lives, enabling them to approach challenges with confidence and make informed decisions in a complex and ever-changing world.

6

Balancing Screen Time and Offline Activities

Balancing screen time and offline activities is crucial for maintaining a healthy and well-rounded lifestyle, especially in today's digital age. Excessive screen time can lead to various issues, such as physical health problems, sleep disturbances, and social disconnection. Here are some practical strategies to help individuals, especially children and teenagers, strike a balance between screen time and offline activities:

Set Clear Boundaries: Establish clear rules and boundaries regarding screen time. Determine specific time limits for various types of screen activities, such as entertainment, education, and social media use.

Designate Screen-Free Zones: Identify certain areas in your home where screens are not allowed, such as the dining room or the bedroom. Creating screen-free zones helps promote offline interactions.

Schedule Screen Time: Create a daily or weekly schedule that allocates dedicated screen time slots for different purposes. This ensures that screen use is intentional and balanced with other activities.

Prioritize Offline Activities: Encourage engagement in offline activities by offering a variety of options, such as sports, hobbies, reading, and outdoor play. Make these activities appealing and accessible.

Lead by Example: Adults should model balanced screen time behavior. When children see adults prioritizing offline activities and managing their screen time, they are more likely to follow suit.

Engage in Family Activities: Plan regular family activities that don't involve screens, such as board games, hiking, cooking, or art projects. These activities foster family bonding and provide screen-free alternatives.

Establish Tech-Free Times: Designate specific times during the day when screens are off-limits, such as during meals, before bedtime, or during designated "unplugged" hours.

Encourage Outdoor Play: Promote outdoor play and physical activities. Spending time in nature and engaging in sports or outdoor games can help counteract the sedentary nature of screen time.

Educate About Screen Time's Impact: Teach children and teenagers about the potential negative effects of excessive screen time on their health, sleep, and overall well-being. Raise awareness about the importance of balance.

Set Screen Time Rules With Input: Involve children and teenagers in the process of setting screen time rules. Encourage them to suggest reasonable limits and participate in creating a family media plan.

Use Screen Time as a Reward: Frame screen time as a reward for completing chores, homework, or other responsibilities. This reinforces the idea that screen time is earned through responsible behavior.

Monitor Content: Be aware of the content that individuals consume during screen time. Ensure that it aligns with age-appropriate and educational choices.

Limit Multitasking: Encourage individuals to focus on one screen activity at a time. Multitasking with screens can lead to reduced attention span and lower productivity.

Provide Educational Screen Time: Encourage the use of educational apps, games, and content during screen time. Balance entertainment with learning opportunities.

Promote Social Interaction: Encourage children and teenagers to maintain face-to-face social interactions with peers and family members. Screen time should not replace real-life relationships.

Regularly Review and Adjust: Periodically review and adjust screen time rules as children grow and their needs change. Flexibility is essential to accommodate evolving interests and responsibilities.

Balancing screen time and offline activities is an ongoing process that requires communication, consistency, and adaptability. By promoting a healthy balance, individuals can enjoy the benefits of technology while also nurturing their physical, social, and emotional well-being.

Balancing screen time with other activities offers numerous benefits for individuals of all ages. While screens can provide valuable information and entertainment, excessive use can have detrimental effects on physical, mental, and social well-being. Here are the benefits of maintaining a balance between screen time and offline activities:

Physical Health: Reduced Sedentary Behavior: Balancing screen time with physical activities like sports, exercise, and outdoor play helps combat the sedentary lifestyle associated with excessive screen use. This promotes better physical fitness and reduces the risk of health issues like obesity.

Mental Well-being: Improved Mental Health: Spending too much time on screens can contribute to stress, anxiety, and depression. Engaging in offline activities such as hobbies, art, and reading can improve mental well-being and provide relaxation.

Cognitive Development: Enhanced Cognitive Skills: Offline activities like puzzles, board games, and reading stimulate critical thinking, problem-solving, and creativity. Balancing screen time with such activities supports cognitive development.

Social Skills: Stronger Interpersonal Connections: Face-to-face interactions with family and friends during offline activities foster better social skills and build stronger relationships. Excessive screen time can lead to social isolation.

Sleep Quality: Improved Sleep: Reducing screen time before bedtime can lead to better sleep quality. The blue light emitted by screens can interfere with sleep patterns, making it important to have screen-free wind-down time.

Academic Success: Enhanced Learning: Balancing screen time with reading, studying, and educational activities can improve academic performance. It allows for focused, uninterrupted learning.

Emotional Regulation: Better Emotional Regulation: Offline activities provide opportunities for emotional expression and regulation, which can be challenging in the online world. Engaging in hobbies or sports can help manage emotions.

Time Management Skills: Development of Time Management: Balancing screen time with offline activities encourages individuals to manage their time effectively. This skill is valuable for both personal and professional life.

Stress Reduction: Stress Reduction: Offline activities like meditation, gardening, or listening to music can reduce stress and promote relaxation, providing a healthy break from screen-related stressors.

Creativity and Imagination: Foster Creativity: Offline activities, such as art, storytelling, and imaginative play, allow individuals to tap into their creativity and imagination, which can be limited by excessive screen consumption.

Physical Development: Healthy Physical Development: For children, balancing screen time with activities like climbing, running, and playing helps develop fine and gross motor skills, coordination, and spatial awareness.

Family Bonding: Stronger Family Bonds: Offline activities like family game nights, cooking together, or outdoor adventures strengthen family bonds and create lasting memories.

Digital Well-being: Better Digital Well-being: Balancing screen time encourages responsible digital citizenship. It helps individuals maintain a healthy relationship with technology, avoid digital addiction, and practice online safety.

Real-world Skills: Acquisition of Real-world Skills: Offline activities often teach practical skills, from cooking and gardening to woodworking and DIY projects, which are valuable in daily life.

Balance and Moderation: Modeling Balance: Balancing screen time with other activities demonstrates the importance of moderation and self-regulation. It helps individuals develop a sense of control over their technology use.

Overall, balancing screen time with offline activities promotes a holistic and well-rounded lifestyle. It contributes to physical, mental, and emotional well-being, fosters personal growth, and enhances the quality of life in the digital age. Encouraging this balance is essential for individuals to thrive in an increasingly screen-centric world.

Finding a healthy screen time balance is essential for maintaining physical and mental well-being in today's digital age. Here are some practical tips to help individuals, parents, and families establish and maintain a balanced approach to screen time:

For Individuals:

Self-Assessment: Reflect on your screen time habits and identify areas where you may be spending excessive time on screens. Be honest with yourself about your usage patterns.

Set Clear Goals: Define clear goals for your screen time. Determine how much time you want to allocate to work, entertainment, socializing, and other online activities.

Use Screen Time Tracking Apps: Utilize screen time tracking apps or built-in features on devices to monitor and analyze your screen time. This provides insights into your usage patterns.

Prioritize Offline Activities: Make a list of offline activities you enjoy, such as hobbies, sports, or reading. Schedule dedicated time for these activities to ensure a balanced routine.

Establish Tech-Free Zones: Designate specific areas or times where screens are not allowed, such as during meals, in the bedroom before bedtime, or during family gatherings.

Set Boundaries: Set specific time limits for different types of screen activities. For example, limit social media use to 30 minutes a day or gaming to an hour on weekends.

Digital Detox: Periodically schedule digital detox days or weekends where you disconnect from screens completely. Use this time to recharge and engage in offline activities.

Practice Mindful Screen Use: Be mindful of your screen time. Ask yourself whether the current screen activity is productive or recreational and whether it aligns with your goals.

Turn Off Non-Essential Notifications: Disable non-essential notifications on your devices to reduce distractions and the temptation to check screens frequently.

Set Screen-Free Times: Establish daily screen-free times, such as the first hour after waking up and the last hour before bedtime, to promote better sleep hygiene.

For Parents and Families:

Lead by Example: Parents should model healthy screen time habits for their children. Children are more likely to follow guidelines if they see adults adhering to them.

Create a Family Media Plan: Develop a family media plan that outlines screen time rules, expectations, and consequences. Include guidelines for all family members.

Discuss the Importance of Balance: Have open and age-appropriate discussions with children about the importance of balancing screen time with other activities, such as schoolwork, chores, and physical play.

Set Screen Time Limits: Establish daily or weekly screen time limits for each family member based on their age, needs, and responsibilities.

Designate Screen-Free Times: Designate certain times and areas of the home as screen-free zones. For example, no screens during family meals or while doing homework.

Plan Family Activities: Plan regular family activities that do not involve screens, such as board games, hiking, cooking, or volunteering together.

Educate About Online Safety: Teach children about online safety, privacy, and the potential risks associated with excessive screen time. Encourage responsible digital citizenship.

Involve Children in Rule Setting: Involve children in the process of setting screen time rules and consequences. This promotes their ownership of the guidelines.

Monitor Content: Keep an eye on the content children are consuming and the websites or apps they use. Ensure age-appropriate and safe content.

Encourage Extracurricular Activities: Encourage children to participate in extracurricular activities like sports, arts, or clubs to balance screen time with real-world experiences.

Remember that finding a healthy screen time balance is an ongoing process that may require adjustments as individuals and families evolve. The goal is to create a balanced lifestyle that fosters physical, mental, and emotional well-being while making the most of the benefits that technology offers.

Engaging children in fun and enriching offline activities is a great way to foster creativity, learning, and social interaction. Here are some enjoyable and educational activity ideas for children:

Art and Craft Projects: Encourage creativity with art and craft activities. Provide supplies like colored paper, markers, crayons, glue, and scissors. Children can make greeting cards, paint, create collages, or try their hand at origami.

Nature Exploration: Explore the outdoors by going on nature hikes, picnics, or simply taking a walk in the park. Collect leaves, rocks, and flowers, and discuss the natural world around you.

Cooking and Baking: Involve children in the kitchen by cooking or baking together. Choose simple recipes for cookies, muffins, or homemade pizza. Kids can measure ingredients, mix, and decorate.

Board Games and Puzzles: Board games and puzzles are excellent for family bonding. Classics like chess, Monopoly, Scrabble, and jigsaw puzzles are both entertaining and mentally stimulating.

Reading Adventures: Visit the library or create a cozy reading nook at home. Encourage children to explore books that match their interests and reading levels. Reading together can be a delightful shared activity.

Gardening: Plant a small garden or maintain potted plants. Children can learn about nature, responsibility, and patience while nurturing their own green space.

Science Experiments: Conduct simple science experiments at home using household items. Try activities like making a volcano with baking soda and vinegar, growing crystals, or exploring static electricity.

Building with Blocks and Legos: Building with blocks, Legos, or other construction toys enhances spatial awareness and fine motor skills. Children can create their structures and inventions.

Arts and Theater: Encourage drama and creativity by putting on a play, puppet show, or talent show at home. Children can design costumes, write scripts, and perform for family members.

Music and Dance: Explore the world of music and dance. Provide musical instruments, have dance parties, or enroll children in music or dance classes if they're interested.

Outdoor Sports and Games: Play outdoor sports like soccer, basketball, or frisbee. Organize family sports tournaments, treasure hunts, or obstacle courses in the backyard.

Journaling and Storytelling: Encourage children to keep journals, write stories, or create their comic books. This activity fosters creativity and writing skills.

Visit Museums and Zoos: Explore local museums, science centers, or zoos. These outings provide educational experiences and stimulate curiosity.

DIY Science Kits: Invest in DIY science kits that come with materials and instructions for exciting experiments. Kits are available for various age levels and interests.

Photography and Nature Observations: Provide children with a camera or smartphone and encourage them to take photos of interesting things they see during nature walks. Discuss their observations afterward.

Community Service Projects: Engage in community service projects together, such as cleaning up a park, volunteering at a local shelter, or organizing a food drive. It teaches empathy and social responsibility.

Stargazing and Astronomy: Spend evenings stargazing and learning about the night sky. Use a telescope or binoculars to identify constellations and planets.

Building Forts and Dens: Let children use blankets, cushions, and furniture to build their forts or dens. These cozy hideaways can be used for reading, imaginative play, or quiet time.

Science and History Documentaries: Watch age-appropriate science and history documentaries together. Discuss the topics and encourage questions.

Yoga and Mindfulness Activities: Practice yoga or mindfulness exercises with children to promote relaxation and emotional well-being. Many resources are available online for guided sessions.

Remember to adapt these activities based on your child's age, interests, and developmental stage. The key is to create a balance of fun and educational experiences that engage their minds and keep them physically active.

7
Tech and Education

The integration of technology into education has transformed the way we teach and learn. In the digital age, technology offers various tools and platforms that enhance educational experiences, expand access to knowledge, and prepare students for a tech-driven future. Here's an exploration of the impact of technology on education:

1. Access to Information: Technology provides immediate access to vast amounts of information and educational resources, breaking down geographical barriers and ensuring equitable access to knowledge.

2. Personalized Learning: Adaptive learning platforms use data and algorithms to personalize instruction, catering to each student's pace and learning style. This individualized approach enhances comprehension and retention.

3. Interactive Learning: Digital tools, such as simulations, virtual labs, and interactive apps, engage students in hands-on learning experiences that promote critical thinking and problem-solving skills.

4. Remote Learning and Flexibility: Online learning platforms and video conferencing tools have made education more flexible, enabling students to access courses and resources remotely, which is particularly valuable during crises like the COVID-19 pandemic.

5. Collaboration and Communication: Technology facilitates collaboration among students and teachers, regardless of location. Virtual classrooms, discussion forums, and collaborative tools enable interactive learning experiences.

6. Enhanced Assessment: Technology offers innovative assessment methods, such as computer-based testing and automated grading, allowing educators to provide timely feedback and assess student progress more efficiently.

7. Global Learning Opportunities: Online courses and platforms connect students with educators and experts from around the world, fostering a global perspective and exposing them to diverse viewpoints.

8. Engaging Multimedia Content: Multimedia elements, like videos, animations, and interactive diagrams, make complex concepts more understandable and engaging, catering to various learning styles.

9. Gamification and EdTech Apps: Gamified learning platforms and educational apps use game elements to make learning enjoyable, motivating students to actively participate and progress.

10. Career Readiness: Educational technology equips students with digital literacy skills and prepares them for careers in technology-driven fields, enhancing their employability.

11. Cost Savings: Digital textbooks and open educational resources (OER) reduce the cost of educational materials, making education more accessible and affordable.

12. Data-Driven Decision-Making: Schools and institutions use data analytics to track student performance, identify areas for improvement, and tailor educational strategies accordingly.

13. Teacher Professional Development: Technology provides teachers with opportunities for continuous professional development, including online courses, webinars, and collaborative platforms for sharing best practices.

14. Inclusion and Accessibility: Assistive technologies and accessibility features ensure that education is inclusive for students with disabilities, accommodating diverse learning needs.

15. Lifelong Learning: Technology encourages a culture of lifelong learning, where individuals of all ages can access educational content and upskill or reskill throughout their lives.

However, it's essential to address challenges like the digital divide, privacy concerns, and the need for responsible technology use. Balancing technology with traditional teaching methods and fostering critical thinking about digital information are also crucial.

Technology has become an integral part of modern education, offering opportunities for innovation, accessibility, and personalized learning. When used thoughtfully and responsibly, technology can empower educators and learners to navigate the ever-evolving landscape of knowledge and skills in the 21st century.

The Role of Technology in Education: Empowering Learners in the Digital Age

Technology has become an integral part of modern education, revolutionizing the way students learn and teachers instruct. Its role in education extends far beyond the use of computers and tablets in classrooms; it encompasses a wide range of tools and strategies that enhance learning, promote accessibility, and prepare students for the challenges of a tech-driven world. Here's an in-depth look at the multifaceted role of technology in education:

1. Access to Information and Resources: Technology provides students with instant access to a wealth of information, from digital libraries and databases to online courses and research materials. This access levels the playing field, ensuring that students from diverse backgrounds have equal opportunities to learn.

2. Personalized Learning: Adaptive learning platforms and educational software use data analytics to tailor instruction to individual students' needs, pace, and learning styles. This personalization enhances comprehension and retention.

3. Interactive Learning Environments: Digital tools, such as simulations, virtual reality, and interactive apps, create engaging and immersive learning experiences. These tools enable students to explore complex concepts hands-on, fostering critical thinking and problem-solving skills.

4. Remote Learning and Flexibility: Online learning platforms and video conferencing tools have made education more flexible and accessible. Students can attend classes, access resources, and collaborate with peers and educators from anywhere, which proved especially valuable during the COVID-19 pandemic.

5. Collaboration and Communication: Technology facilitates collaboration among students and teachers through virtual classrooms, discussion forums, collaborative documents, and video conferencing. These tools promote interactive learning experiences and communication skills.

6. Enhanced Assessment: Technology offers innovative assessment methods, including computer-based testing and automated grading. These tools allow educators to provide timely feedback and gain insights into student progress.

7. Global Learning Opportunities: Online courses and platforms connect students with educators and experts from around the world, providing exposure to diverse perspectives and fostering a global mindset.

8. Gamification and Educational Apps: Gamified learning platforms and educational apps leverage game elements to make learning enjoyable and motivating. They encourage active participation and progress tracking.

9. Cost Savings: Digital textbooks, open educational resources (OER), and online courses reduce the cost of educational materials, making education more accessible and affordable.

10. Career Readiness: Educational technology equips students with digital literacy skills and prepares them for careers in technology-driven fields, enhancing their employability.

11. Data-Driven Decision-Making: Schools and institutions use data analytics to track student performance, identify areas for improvement, and tailor educational strategies accordingly.

12. Teacher Professional Development: Technology provides teachers with opportunities for continuous professional development through online courses, webinars, and collaborative platforms for sharing best practices.

13. Inclusion and Accessibility: Assistive technologies and accessibility features ensure that education is inclusive for students with disabilities, accommodating diverse learning needs.

14. Lifelong Learning: Technology encourages a culture of lifelong learning, allowing individuals of all ages to access educational content and upskill or reskill throughout their lives.

Even if technology has a transformational effect on education, issues including the digital divide, privacy concerns, and the requirement for responsible technology use must be addressed. A well-rounded education also depends on striking a balance between traditional teaching techniques and technology. In general, a new era of education has been brought about by technology, which presents chances for creativity, accessibility, and customized learning. When used wisely, it gives teachers and students the ability to negotiate the constantly changing terrain of 21st-century knowledge and abilities.

Effective use of technology in education necessitates a deliberate and planned approach that optimizes its advantages while minimizing any potential downsides. The following recommendations will assist educators, learners of all ages, and students in making the most of technology in the classroom

For Students:

> Set Clear Goals: Define your learning objectives. Understand what you want to achieve with the use of technology, whether it's mastering a subject, improving a skill, or accessing specific resources.

> Choose Appropriate Tools: Select technology tools and apps that align with your learning goals. Research and experiment with various platforms to find the ones that work best for you.

> Manage Screen Time: Set boundaries for screen time to prevent digital burnout and distractions. Use apps or features that track your screen time to stay mindful of usage.

> Stay Organized: Use digital tools like calendars, to-do lists, and note-taking apps to stay organized. These tools can help you manage assignments, deadlines, and study schedules.

> Active Learning: Engage actively with technology rather than passively consuming content. Participate in online discussions, solve problems interactively, and create your content where possible.

> Seek Help and Support: Don't hesitate to ask for help when you encounter technical issues or struggle with learning materials. Many educational institutions offer tech support, and online communities can provide valuable assistance.

> Practice Digital Literacy: Develop digital literacy skills, including critical thinking, fact-checking, and online etiquette. Be discerning when evaluating online sources and information.

Collaborate Online: Collaborate with peers using online platforms for group projects, study sessions, and discussions. Virtual teamwork can enhance your understanding of topics.

Regularly Back Up Work: Save your work in multiple locations or cloud storage to prevent data loss. Regularly back up important documents and assignments.

For Learners of All Ages:

Practice Time Management: Develop effective time management skills to balance online learning with other responsibilities. Create a daily or weekly schedule that allocates dedicated study time.

Stay Informed: Stay informed about emerging technologies and their potential impact on education. Be open to exploring new tools and approaches.

Online Etiquette: Practice good online etiquette and respectful communication when interacting with peers, teachers, or online communities.

Critical Thinking: Cultivate critical thinking skills to evaluate the credibility and quality of online information. Verify sources and question assumptions.

Seek Help When Needed: If you encounter challenges with technology or your learning experience, don't hesitate to seek help from teachers, tech support, or mentors.

Reflect and Adapt: Periodically reflect on your tech-enhanced learning experiences. Assess what's working well and make adjustments as needed to improve your learning journey.

Balance Technology Use: Maintain a healthy balance between technology use for learning and offline activities to support physical and mental well-being.

Effective use of technology in the classroom is a continuous process that calls for self-control, flexibility, and a commitment to learning objectives. Accept technology as a useful tool to improve learning, but always be aware of how it fits into your overall learning approach.

In the current digital era, technology can be a useful tool for parenting. It can support children's wellbeing and assist parents in being informed, connected, and organized. Here are a few strategies for parents to employ technology in their parenting:

Online Parenting Resources: Utilize websites, forums, and social media groups dedicated to parenting. These platforms provide a wealth of information, advice, and support from other parents who have experienced similar challenges.

Parenting Apps: There are numerous parenting apps available that can assist with various aspects of parenting. These apps can help track feeding and sleeping schedules for infants, manage family calendars, and offer tips and advice.

Educational Apps and Games: Use educational apps and games to promote learning and skill development in a fun and interactive way. Many apps are designed to support early childhood education and cognitive development.

Online Safety Tools: Implement parental control and monitoring software to ensure your child's online safety. These tools help manage screen time, filter content, and track online activities.

Communication Tools: Stay connected with your children through messaging apps, video calls, and social media. These tools can facilitate communication when you're apart and strengthen your bond.

Health and Wellness Apps: Use health and wellness apps to track your child's growth, nutrition, and medical appointments. These apps can provide reminders and guidance for maintaining your child's well-being.

Parenting Blogs and Podcasts: Follow parenting blogs and podcasts to access expert advice, parenting tips, and insights into child development. These resources can keep you informed and provide guidance on various parenting topics.

Homework and Learning Platforms: Stay involved in your child's education by using online platforms that provide access to homework assignments, grades, and teacher communication. Many schools use these tools to keep parents informed and engaged.

Digital Storytelling: Create digital photo albums, videos, and digital scrapbooks to capture precious family moments and memories. Share these with extended family members to maintain connections.

Family Organization Apps: Use family organization apps to coordinate schedules, track appointments, and manage to-do lists. These apps help streamline household responsibilities and reduce stress.

Parental Support Groups: Participate in online support groups or forums specifically for parents facing similar challenges, such as parenting a child with special needs or dealing with specific health concerns.

Learning and Skill Development Tools: Encourage your child's learning and skill development through educational websites and online courses. Platforms like Khan Academy and Coursera offer a wide range of resources for learners of all ages.

Parental Control Features on Devices: Enable parental control features on devices to limit screen time, control access to apps and content, and set age-appropriate restrictions.

Online Safety Education: Teach your children about online safety, responsible internet use, and the potential risks associated with technology. Encourage open communication about their online experiences.

Digital Parenting Courses: Consider enrolling in digital parenting courses or workshops to enhance your understanding of technology's impact on child development and effective parenting strategies in the digital age.

While technology can be a valuable resource for parenting, it's crucial to strike a balance and use it mindfully. Be aware of the potential risks and challenges associated with technology use by both parents and children, and prioritize quality family time and face-to-face interactions. Effective parenting with technology involves using these tools as aids in your parenting journey, not as substitutes for active and engaged parenting.

Certainly! There are numerous educational apps and websites available for learners of all ages and interests. Whether you're a student looking to enhance your knowledge or a parent seeking educational resources for your child, here are some popular platforms and websites:

For K-12 Education:

Khan Academy: Offers free online courses in math, science, economics, and humanities. It's a great resource for students of all ages.

EdX: Provides access to courses from top universities and institutions worldwide. Many courses are free, and you can receive certificates for completing them.

PBS LearningMedia: Offers free lesson plans, videos, and interactive games for educators, parents, and students.

National Geographic Kids: Features educational games, videos, and articles covering a wide range of topics from geography to science.

Scholastic: Provides resources for teachers, parents, and students, including book lists, educational games, and lesson plans.

For College and University Students:

Coursera: Offers a wide range of courses from universities and institutions worldwide. Many courses are free, but you can also earn certificates and degrees for a fee.

edX: Similar to Coursera, edX offers online courses from universities and institutions. You can audit courses for free or pay for certificates.

MIT OpenCourseWare: Provides free access to a vast collection of MIT course materials, including lecture notes, assignments, and exams.

Quizlet: A study platform that offers flashcards, quizzes, and study games for a wide range of subjects.

Google Scholar: A free search engine for scholarly articles, theses, books, and conference papers.

For Skill Development and Professional Learning:

LinkedIn Learning: Provides a vast library of courses on topics like business, technology, and creative skills. It's ideal for professional development.

Duolingo: A popular language learning app that offers courses in multiple languages. It's gamified and suitable for all ages.

Codecademy: An interactive platform for learning programming languages and web development skills.

Skillshare: Offers classes on various creative and entrepreneurial skills, from graphic design to digital marketing.

TED-Ed: Features a library of educational videos and lessons on a wide range of topics delivered by experts and educators.

For Young Children:

ABCmouse: An early learning app and website that covers math, reading, science, and art for children ages 2-8.

Starfall: Offers free games, activities, and phonics lessons to help young children with reading and math.

Sesame Street:

Sesame Street's official website offers educational games, videos, and printable activities for preschoolers.

These resources cover a wide range of educational needs and age groups. Whether you're looking to supplement your formal education, acquire new skills, or provide educational content for your children, you'll find valuable resources among these websites and apps.

8

Cyberbullying and Online Behavior

Cyberbullying is a serious concern in today's digital age, affecting individuals, especially children and adolescents, who engage in online communication and social media. It involves the use of digital platforms to harass, threaten, or intimidate others, causing emotional distress and harm. Understanding cyberbullying and promoting positive online behavior are essential for a safer and more inclusive digital environment.

Understanding Cyberbullying:

> **Types of Cyberbullying:** Cyberbullying can take various forms, including:
>
> > Harassment: Repeated offensive messages or threats.
> >
> > Flaming: Posting derogatory comments or insults.
> >
> > Doxxing: Sharing personal information without consent.
> >
> > Outing: Publicly revealing someone's private information.
> >
> > Impersonation: Pretending to be someone else online.
> >
> > Exclusion: Deliberately excluding or isolating someone online.
>
> **Effects of Cyberbullying:** Cyberbullying can have severe consequences, leading to emotional distress, depression, anxiety, and even physical harm. Victims may experience academic or professional setbacks and may become socially withdrawn.
>
> **The Role of Bystanders:** Bystanders, individuals who witness cyberbullying, play a crucial role. They can

intervene, support the victim, or report the incident to authorities.

Preventing Cyberbullying:

Education and Awareness: Promote awareness of cyberbullying through educational programs. Teach children and adolescents about online etiquette, empathy, and the potential consequences of harmful online behavior.

Open Communication: Encourage open communication between parents, caregivers, and children. Create a safe space for children to share their online experiences and concerns.

Privacy Settings: Teach individuals to use privacy settings on social media and online platforms to control who can access their information.

Online Etiquette: Promote respectful online behavior and remind individuals that their online actions have real-world consequences.

Reporting Mechanisms: Ensure that children and adults know reporting mechanisms on social media platforms and websites. Encourage them to report instances of cyberbullying.

Digital Empowerment: Empower individuals with the skills to protect themselves online, including recognizing scams, managing online relationships, and understanding privacy settings.

Addressing Cyberbullying:

Document Evidence: If someone is experiencing cyberbullying, document the evidence, including screenshots and timestamps. This can be helpful when reporting incidents.

Report to Authorities: Report cyberbullying to appropriate authorities, such as school administrators, social media platforms, or law enforcement, depending on the severity.

Support Victims: Offer emotional support to victims of cyberbullying. Let them know they are not alone and that help is available.

Consequences for Perpetrators: Perpetrators of cyberbullying should face appropriate consequences, which may include school disciplinary actions or legal repercussions.

Online Safety Measures: Encourage individuals to use safety measures like blocking, unfriending, or setting accounts to private if they feel threatened or harassed.

Promote Positive Online Communities: Foster positive online environments that prioritize inclusivity, empathy, and respectful communication.

Mental Health Support: Ensure that individuals who experience cyberbullying have access to mental health support and counseling services.

Remember that preventing and addressing cyberbullying requires a collective effort from parents, educators, caregivers, and online communities. It's essential to promote a culture of respect and empathy in both the digital and physical worlds, ensuring that individuals can enjoy the benefits of online connectivity without fear of harassment or harm.

Cyberbullying and inappropriate online behavior pose significant risks to individuals, particularly children, adolescents, and vulnerable populations. Understanding these risks is crucial for creating a safer and more respectful digital environment. Here are the key risks associated with cyberbullying and inappropriate online behavior:

Emotional and Psychological Harm:

> **Depression and Anxiety:** Cyberbullying can lead to depression, anxiety, and other mental health issues, especially in victims who feel isolated or helpless.

> **Low Self-Esteem:** Inappropriate online behavior, including derogatory comments and cyberbullying, can erode self-esteem and self-worth, particularly in young people.

Social Isolation:

Withdrawal: Victims of cyberbullying may withdraw from social interactions, both online and offline, due to fear, embarrassment, or shame.

Loss of Friends: Inappropriate behavior can lead to losing friends and damage one's reputation, making it difficult to maintain social relationships.

Academic and Professional Consequences:

Decline in Performance: Cyberbullying victims may experience a decline in academic or professional performance, affecting their long-term prospects.

Damage to Career: Inappropriate online behavior, including posting compromising content, can harm one's career prospects and reputation.

Physical Health Impacts:

Stress-Related Health Issues: Prolonged exposure to cyberbullying can lead to physical health issues, such as headaches, sleep disturbances, and even stress-related illnesses.

Self-Harm and Suicide: In extreme cases, cyberbullying can drive individuals to self-harm or suicide as they struggle to cope with the emotional pain.

Privacy Breaches:

Personal Information Exposure: Inappropriate behavior may involve the sharing of personal information, leading to identity theft, harassment, or stalking.

Digital Blackmail: Perpetrators may engage in digital blackmail, threatening to expose compromising content unless certain demands are met.

Legal and Criminal Consequences:

Legal Action: In some cases, inappropriate online behavior can lead to legal action, including charges of harassment, defamation, or violating privacy laws.

Criminal Records: Cyberbullying that escalates to criminal behavior, such as threats or hate crimes, can result in criminal records and penalties.

Impact on Mental Well-Being:

Perpetrators' Guilt: Those engaging in cyberbullying may experience guilt, anxiety, and legal consequences if their actions are discovered.

Negative Online Reputation: Inappropriate online behavior can tarnish one's online reputation, affecting personal and professional relationships.

Safety Risks:

Physical Harm: In extreme cases, cyberbullying may escalate to physical harm or offline harassment if the perpetrator knows the victim's location.

Predatory Behavior: Online predators may exploit victims through grooming, manipulation, or coercion.

Spread of Harmful Content:

Viral Impact: Harmful content, including cyberbullying messages, can spread rapidly online, causing widespread damage.

Permanent Digital Footprint: Inappropriate online behavior can leave a permanent digital footprint, making it challenging to move past past mistakes.

It's essential to address these risks proactively by promoting digital literacy, responsible online behavior, and open communication among individuals, families, educators, and online communities. By raising awareness about the consequences of cyberbullying and inappropriate online behavior, we can work towards creating a safer and more respectful digital environment for everyone.

Addressing and preventing cyberbullying and inappropriate online behavior requires a multi-faceted approach involving individuals, families, schools, and online communities. Here is some advice on how to address and prevent these issues:

For Individuals:

> **Think Before You Post:** Encourage self-reflection and mindfulness before sharing content online. Remind individuals that once something is online, it may be permanent.

> **Practice Digital Empathy:** Promote empathy by encouraging individuals to consider how their online actions and words may affect others. Encourage kindness and respect in online interactions.

> **Use Privacy Settings:** Teach individuals, especially children and teens, to review and use privacy settings on social media platforms and apps to control who can access their information.

> **Recognize Warning Signs:** Educate individuals about the signs of cyberbullying, both as potential victims and bystanders. Encourage them to report any concerning behavior.

For Parents and Caregivers:

> **Open Communication:** Maintain open and non-judgmental communication with your children about their online experiences. Create a safe space for them to share any concerns.

> **Set Screen Time Limits:** Establish screen time limits and encourage a healthy balance between online and offline activities like physical exercise, hobbies, and face-to-face interactions.

> **Educate About Online Safety:** Teach children about online safety, including the risks of sharing personal

information, meeting strangers online, and the importance of strong, unique passwords.

Monitor Online Activities: Monitor your child's online activities, mainly if they are younger or less experienced with technology. Keep an eye on their social media accounts and friend lists.

Report and Document: Encourage your child to report any cyberbullying incidents to you and their school if appropriate. Help them document evidence, such as screenshots.

For Schools and Educators:

Implement Anti-Bullying Programs: Schools should have anti-bullying programs that include cyberbullying awareness and prevention. Create a safe reporting mechanism for students.

Promote Digital Literacy: Integrate digital literacy education into the curriculum to teach students critical thinking, online etiquette, and responsible technology use.

Teacher Training: Provide teachers with training on recognizing and addressing cyberbullying. Encourage them to create a supportive classroom environment.

For Online Communities:

Community Guidelines: Establish clear and enforceable community guidelines that promote respectful behavior and prohibit harassment and hate speech.

Moderation: Employ active moderation on social media platforms, forums, and websites to remove inappropriate content and address violations promptly.

Reporting Mechanisms: Make it easy for users to report abusive behavior. Take reports seriously and investigate them promptly.

Public Awareness Campaigns: Run public awareness campaigns about online safety, cyberbullying, and the importance of reporting inappropriate behavior.

For Everyone:

> **Support Victims:** If you witness cyberbullying, offer support to the victim and report the incident. Bystanders can play a vital role in ending online harassment.

> **Seek Help:** If you or someone you know is experiencing cyberbullying or inappropriate online behavior, seek help from trusted adults, counselors, or mental health professionals.

Addressing and preventing cyberbullying and inappropriate online behavior requires collective efforts to create a safer and more respectful digital environment. By fostering responsible online behavior, raising awareness, and providing support to those affected, we can work together to reduce the harm caused by these issues.

Fostering positive online behavior is essential for creating a respectful and inclusive digital environment. Whether you're a parent, educator, or community leader, here are strategies to promote positive online behavior:

For Parents and Caregivers:

> **Set a Good Example:** Model positive online behavior for your children. Show them how to interact respectfully and empathetically with others.

> **Open Communication:** Maintain open and honest communication with your children about their online experiences. Encourage them to share both positive and negative encounters.

> **Educate About Cyber Etiquette:** Teach your children about online etiquette, emphasizing the importance of politeness, empathy, and respect when communicating online.

> **Emphasize Privacy and Security:** Explain the significance of protecting personal information online and guide your children on how to set strong, unique passwords.

> **Promote Critical Thinking:** Encourage critical thinking skills by discussing the credibility of online sources and

helping your children discern between reliable and unreliable information.

Teach Responsible Sharing: Emphasize responsible content sharing. Teach children that once something is online, it can be challenging to remove or control.

Monitor and Guide: Monitor your child's online activities while respecting their privacy. Provide guidance when needed, particularly for younger children.

Positive Reinforcement: Acknowledge and reward positive online behavior. Praise your children for being kind and respectful in their online interactions.

For Educators:

Digital Literacy Curriculum: Incorporate digital literacy education into the curriculum, focusing on topics like online etiquette, critical thinking, and responsible digital citizenship.

Classroom Discussions: Foster classroom discussions about online behavior, cyberbullying, and the impact of online actions on individuals and communities.

Role-Playing Exercises: Conduct role-playing exercises to help students practice responding to cyberbullying and resolving online conflicts peacefully.

Online Safety Workshops: Organize workshops or guest speakers to address online safety, digital ethics, and responsible technology use.

For Online Communities:

Community Guidelines: Develop and enforce clear community guidelines that promote respectful behavior and prohibit harassment, hate speech, and discrimination.

Active Moderation: Implement active moderation to monitor and remove inappropriate content. Ensure that reported violations are addressed promptly.

Positive Behavior Recognition: Recognize and reward positive online behavior within the community. Highlight individuals who contribute positively.

For Everyone:

Digital Empathy: Encourage digital empathy by reminding individuals to consider the feelings and perspectives of others before posting or commenting.

Think Before You Share: Promote critical thinking before sharing content online. Encourage individuals to verify information and consider the potential impact of their posts.

Report Inappropriate Behavior: Encourage individuals to report instances of cyberbullying or inappropriate online behavior to platform moderators or authorities when necessary.

Conflict Resolution Skills: Teach conflict resolution skills, emphasizing the importance of resolving disagreements through respectful dialogue rather than hostility.

Online Positivity Campaigns: Engage in or support online positivity campaigns that promote kindness, empathy, and respectful communication.

Fostering positive online behavior is an ongoing effort that requires a collective commitment from parents, educators, online communities, and individuals themselves. By nurturing a culture of respect, empathy, and responsible digital citizenship, we can create a more welcoming and constructive online world for everyone

Open Communication

Open communication is a fundamental aspect of healthy relationships, whether they are between parents and children, partners, friends, or colleagues. Effective communication fosters understanding, trust, and mutual respect. Here are some strategies and principles to promote open communication:

Active Listening: Actively listen when others are speaking. Avoid interrupting or formulating your response while they are talking.

Show that you are fully engaged and interested in what they are saying.

Empathy: Try to understand others' perspectives and feelings. Empathize with their emotions and experiences, even if you don't necessarily agree with them.

Use "I" Statements: Express your thoughts, feelings, and concerns using "I" statements. For example, say, "I feel frustrated when..." instead of "You always do..."

Avoid Blame and Accusations: Instead of blaming or accusing others, focus on the specific behaviors or actions that are causing issues. Address the problem, not the person.

Non-Verbal Communication: Pay attention to non-verbal cues like body language, facial expressions, and tone of voice. These can convey emotions and messages that words alone may not.

Be Patient: Give others the time they need to express themselves fully. Don't rush the conversation, especially when discussing sensitive topics.

Ask Open-Ended Questions: Encourage deeper discussions by asking open-ended questions that require more than a simple "yes" or "no" response.

Respect Differences: Recognize that people have different backgrounds, perspectives, and communication styles. Be respectful of these differences.

Validate Feelings: Acknowledge and validate others' feelings, even if you don't share the same emotions. For example, you can say, "I understand that you're feeling upset about this."

Avoid Assumptions: - Don't assume you know what someone is thinking or feeling. Ask clarifying questions to ensure you have a complete understanding.

Use Technology Mindfully: - When communicating through digital means, be mindful of tone and context. Messages can be misinterpreted, so consider the potential impact of your words.

Create a Safe Space: - Foster an environment where people feel safe to express themselves without fear of judgment or ridicule. Encourage open dialogue and mutual respect.

Stay Calm: - In emotionally charged conversations, try to remain calm and composed. Emotional reactions can hinder productive communication.

Problem-Solving Orientation: - Approach conflicts with a problem-solving mindset. Focus on finding solutions rather than dwelling on the issue itself.

Seek Feedback: - Encourage feedback from others about your communication style. Ask for constructive criticism and be open to making improvements.

Regular Check-Ins: - Make time for regular check-ins with the people important to you. These can be informal conversations to maintain and strengthen your relationships.

Apologize When Necessary: - If you make a mistake or say something hurtful, apologize sincerely. Taking responsibility for your words and actions is a sign of maturity.

Open communication is a skill that can be developed and improved over time. By actively practicing these principles and strategies, you can enhance your ability to connect with others, resolve conflicts, and build stronger, more meaningful relationships in both your personal and professional life.

Importance of open and honest communication

Open and honest communication is the cornerstone of healthy and thriving relationships, both in personal and professional spheres. Its significance cannot be overstated, as it serves as the foundation for trust, understanding, and meaningful connections. Here's why open and honest communication is so crucial:

Builds Trust: Openness and honesty breed trust. When individuals consistently share their thoughts, feelings, and intentions truthfully, others can rely on their words and actions.

Strengthens Relationships: Strong bonds are forged through open and honest communication. It allows people to connect on a deeper level, fostering intimacy and emotional closeness.

Resolves Conflicts: Transparent communication enables the resolution of conflicts in a constructive manner. It encourages discussion, compromise, and finding common ground.

Promotes Understanding: Through open communication, people gain insights into each other's perspectives, needs, and motivations. This understanding leads to empathy and reduced misunderstandings.

Each other's needs and work Fosters Collaboration: In professional settings, open communication is essential for teamwork and collaboration. It ensures that everyone is on the same page and working towards common goals.

Boosts Productivity: Effective communication streamlines processes and minimizes errors and miscommunications. It allows tasks to be completed more efficiently.

Encourages Innovation: An open environment where ideas and feedback are freely shared fosters creativity and innovation. People feel more comfortable contributing their thoughts.

Enhances Personal Growth: Honest self-expression facilitates personal growth. It allows individuals to acknowledge their strengths and weaknesses, seek feedback, and make necessary improvements.

Supports Mental Health: Sharing one's feelings and struggles through open communication can alleviate emotional burdens. It promotes mental well-being and reduces stress.

Prevents Resentment: When concerns or grievances are communicated promptly, they can be addressed and resolved before they escalate into long-lasting resentment.

Improves Decision-Making: Well-informed decisions are made when all relevant information is openly discussed and considered. This applies to both personal and professional choices.

Strengthens Accountability: Honest communication encourages accountability for one's words and actions.

People are more likely to take responsibility for their behavior when they know it's valued.

Builds a Support System: In personal relationships, open communication creates a support system where individuals can share their joys and sorrows, knowing they will be heard and understood.

Facilitates Effective Parenting: Parents who communicate openly and honestly with their children build strong, trusting relationships. It also helps in teaching children important life skills.

Promotes Ethical Behavior: Ethical conduct is reinforced when individuals communicate honestly and transparently. It discourages deception and unethical practices.

Strengthens Organizational Culture: In the workplace, open communication is vital for creating a positive organizational culture that values transparency, feedback, and employee well-being.

Enhances Negotiation Skills: Openness in negotiations leads to more successful outcomes. Parties can better understand towards mutually beneficial agreements.

In summary, open and honest communication is the lifeblood of meaningful relationships, effective collaboration, and personal growth. It promotes trust, understanding, and emotional well-being while reducing conflict and misunderstandings. As such, it is a skill worth cultivating and prioritizing in all aspects of life.

Tips for talking to kids about technology and digital well-being.

Talking to kids about technology and digital well-being is crucial in today's digital age. Here are some tips to help parents and caregivers have productive and meaningful conversations with children about technology and its impact on their well-being:

Start Early: Begin discussions about technology and digital well-being at a young age. As soon as children start using digital devices, introduce age-appropriate conversations about responsible tech use.

Be a Role Model: Demonstrate healthy technology habits by modeling responsible screen time, balanced device use, and respectful online behavior. Children often learn by observing their parents.

Use Age-Appropriate Language: Tailor your conversations to your child's age and developmental stage. Use language and concepts they can understand and relate to.

Foster Openness: Create an environment where children feel comfortable discussing their digital experiences, concerns, and questions without fear of judgment or punishment.

Emphasize Balance: Teach the importance of balancing screen time with offline activities, such as outdoor play, reading, hobbies, and spending time with family and friends.

Discuss Online Safety: Explain the basics of online safety, including not sharing personal information, being cautious about strangers online, and recognizing potential dangers.

Address Cyberbullying and Digital Etiquette: Discuss the importance of treating others with kindness and respect online, and how to recognize and respond to cyberbullying.

Set Family Rules: Establish clear family rules and guidelines for technology use, including screen time limits, appropriate apps and websites, and device-free zones.

Collaborate on Tech Decisions: Involve children in decisions about their technology use. Ask for their input when setting rules and boundaries.

Explain Consequences: Discuss the potential consequences of excessive screen time, such as reduced sleep, physical health issues, and the impact on academic performance.

Teach Critical Thinking: Help children develop critical thinking skills to assess the reliability of online information and question the content they encounter.

Discuss Mental Health: Talk about the impact of screen time on mental health, emphasizing the importance of taking breaks, managing stress, and seeking support if needed.

Encourage Digital Detox: Suggest periodic digital detoxes or breaks to unplug and reconnect with the real world.

Stay Informed: Keep up-to-date with the latest apps, social media trends, and online platforms your children may be using. This enables you to have informed conversations.

Be Patient and Supportive: Understand that technology is an integral part of children's lives. Be patient, empathetic, and supportive as they navigate the digital world.

Use Real-Life Examples: Share stories or news articles about digital well-being, cyberbullying incidents, or the consequences of excessive screen time to illustrate important points.

Promote Creativity: Encourage children to use technology for creative and educational purposes, such as exploring new hobbies, learning coding, or creating digital art.

Reinforce Positive Behavior: Acknowledge and praise responsible tech use and respectful online behavior when you observe it.

Stay Updated Together: Explore new apps, games, and websites together as a way to bond and understand your child's digital interests.

Seek Professional Help if Needed: If you notice signs of technology addiction or severe online-related issues, consult a mental health professional or counselor for guidance.

Remember that ongoing conversations about technology and digital well-being are essential. Keep the lines of communication open, adapt your discussions to your child's changing needs, and be a supportive guide as they navigate the digital world approaches for addressing concerns and questions

Addressing concerns and questions that children have about technology and digital well-being requires a thoughtful and supportive approach. Here are some strategies to effectively address their inquiries and worries:

Active Listening: Begin by actively listening to your child's concerns or questions without interruption. This shows that you value their thoughts and feelings.

Validate Their Feelings: Acknowledge your child's emotions and let them know that it's okay to have concerns or questions about technology. Validating their feelings can help them feel understood and accepted.

Empathize: Put yourself in your child's shoes and empathize with their perspective. Understand that their concerns may be genuine and significant to them.

Offer Age-Appropriate Answers: Tailor your responses to your child's age and developmental stage. Provide explanations and information that are appropriate and understandable for their level of comprehension.

Provide Balanced Information: Offer a balanced view of technology, highlighting both its advantages and potential risks. Emphasize that technology can be a valuable tool when used responsibly.

Address Safety Concerns: If your child's concerns relate to online safety or cyberbullying, provide practical advice on how to protect themselves and seek help when needed.

Share Your Own Experiences: Share stories or examples from your own life where you faced similar concerns or questions about technology. This can help your child see that they are not alone in their worries.

Explore Together: If your child has specific questions about a digital platform or app, explore it together. This hands-on approach can help demystify technology and ease concerns.

Teach Critical Thinking: Help your child develop critical thinking skills to evaluate the credibility of online information and make informed decisions.

Foster Problem-Solving: - Encourage your child to brainstorm solutions to their concerns or questions. This empowers them to take an active role in addressing their worries.

Set Boundaries: - If necessary, establish clear boundaries or guidelines for technology use that address your child's concerns and align with your family's values.

Reassure Your Availability: - Let your child know that they can always come to you with questions or concerns about technology, and that you will be there to support them.

Seek Expert Advice: - If you're unsure about how to address a particular concern, don't hesitate to seek advice from experts, such as pediatricians, child psychologists, or educators.

Monitor and Follow Up: - After addressing a concern or question, continue to monitor your child's digital activities and well-being. Follow up with them periodically to ensure that their worries have been alleviated.

Encourage Responsible Tech Use: - Promote responsible tech use and digital citizenship. Teach your child how to make positive choices online and be a responsible digital citizen.

Share Resources: - Provide age-appropriate books, websites, or educational resources that can help answer your child's questions and address their concerns about technology.

Lead by Example: - Demonstrate responsible and balanced tech use in your own life. Children often learn best by observing the behavior of trusted adults.

Be Patient: - Some concerns and questions may require time to address fully. Be patient and continue the dialogue as needed.

Remember that open and ongoing communication is key. By addressing your child's concerns and questions about technology in a supportive and understanding manner, you can help them navigate the digital world with confidence and responsibility

10

Being a Role Model

Being a role model when it comes to technology and digital well-being is a powerful way to influence children and young people positively. Here's an elaboration on how to be an effective role model in the digital age:

Balanced Device Use: Demonstrate a balanced approach to technology use. Set boundaries for your screen time and adhere to them. Show that technology is a tool for productivity and enjoyment but not an all-consuming activity.

Respectful Online Behavior: Model respectful and considerate online behavior. Display empathy and kindness in your digital interactions, whether through emails, social media, or online forums.

Privacy Management: Teach your children about online privacy and security by example. Use strong and unique passwords, enable two-factor authentication, and protect your personal information online.

Critical Thinking: Encourage critical thinking skills. Discuss news articles or social media posts with your child, pointing out how to verify information, recognize bias, and think critically about online content.

Limit Multitasking: Avoid excessive multitasking when using devices. Show that focusing on one task at a time can lead to better productivity and understanding.

Respect Family Rules: Adhere to the same technology rules and guidelines you establish for your children. Consistency sends a clear message about the importance of responsible tech use.

Digital Detox: Practice digital detoxes periodically. Share with your children that taking breaks from screens is essential for mental and physical well-being.

Engage in Offline Activities: Showcase the importance of offline activities. Spend quality time together as a family engaging in hobbies, outdoor play, reading, or other non-digital pursuits.

Continuous Learning: Demonstrate a willingness to learn about new technologies and digital trends alongside your child. Show that learning is a lifelong process, even in the digital realm.

Media Literacy: Teach your child how to critically analyze advertisements, news stories, and other media content. Discuss the techniques used to persuade or manipulate.

Digital Boundaries: Set clear digital boundaries for yourself, such as not checking work emails during family time or not using your phone during meals. Explain the importance of these boundaries.

Online Safety: Model safe online practices by avoiding suspicious websites and being cautious when sharing personal information. Emphasize that online safety is a priority.

Conflict Resolution: Demonstrate conflict resolution in digital interactions. If you encounter online disagreements or negativity, show how to address them respectfully or disengage when necessary.

Seek Help When Needed: If you encounter challenges related to technology, such as cyberbullying or online harassment, seek help and support as needed. Show that it's okay to ask for assistance.

Open Communication: Maintain open and honest communication with your child about your own technology experiences, including any mistakes or challenges you've faced. Encourage them to share their own experiences.

Being a role model in the digital age is about more than just setting rules and restrictions. It's about embodying the values and behaviors you want to instill in your children when it comes to responsible, respectful, and balanced technology use. Your actions and attitudes have a profound impact on their own attitudes and behaviors, so strive to be a positive digital role model they can emulate.

The importance of parents being tech role models

The importance of parents being tech role models cannot be overstated in today's digital age. Parents play a crucial role in shaping their children's attitudes and behaviors towards technology and digital well-being. Here's why being a tech role model is of paramount importance:

Influence and Imitation: Children naturally look up to their parents as role models. They observe and emulate their parents' behaviors, including how they use technology. If parents demonstrate responsible and balanced tech use, children are more likely to do the same.

Establishing Healthy Habits: Parents who model healthy technology habits set the foundation for their children to develop responsible and balanced tech habits. This includes setting screen time limits, practicing digital etiquette, and valuing face-to-face interactions.

Digital Literacy: Parents who actively engage with technology and teach their children about it contribute to their digital literacy. They can guide children in navigating the digital world, distinguishing reliable information from misinformation, and developing critical thinking skills.

Online Safety: Tech-savvy parents are better equipped to teach their children about online safety. They can provide guidance on recognizing potential risks, protecting personal information, and responding to cyberbullying or inappropriate online behavior.

Communication: Modeling open and honest communication about technology fosters trust and encourages children to approach their parents with questions, concerns, or problems related to their digital experiences. This ongoing dialogue is crucial for maintaining a strong parent-child connection.

Setting Boundaries: Parents who set and adhere to technology-related rules and boundaries demonstrate consistency and accountability. This helps children understand the importance of adhering to these rules themselves.

Digital Citizenship: Being a responsible digital citizen extends beyond personal behavior. Parents who model positive online interactions, such as respectful communication and empathy, help shape their children's understanding of digital citizenship.

Balance: Demonstrating a balance between technology use and offline activities underscores the importance of well-rounded living. Children learn that technology is a valuable tool but should not dominate their lives.

Adaptability: Technology is constantly evolving, and parents who embrace ongoing learning and adaptation to new digital tools and platforms demonstrate the importance of staying current and adapting to change.

Mental Well-Being: Parents who prioritize mental well-being and practice digital detoxes or mindfulness in their tech use convey the significance of maintaining a healthy relationship with technology for overall mental health.

Future Success: In today's digital-driven world, digital literacy and responsible tech use are essential skills for future success. Parents who model these skills help prepare their children for academic and professional success.

Bonding and Quality Time: Parents who engage in technology-related activities with their children, such as playing educational apps or exploring creative projects, strengthen their bonds and create opportunities for quality time together.

In summary, parents serve as the primary role models for their children in all aspects of life, including technology and digital well-being. By embodying responsible, respectful, and balanced tech use, parents can positively influence their children's digital habits, prepare them for the digital world, and strengthen their overall well-being.

Responsible tech use by parents

Responsible tech use by parents is not only important for their own well-being but also sets a powerful example for their children. Here are some key aspects of responsible tech use by parents:

Setting Boundaries: Establish clear boundaries for your own tech use. Determine specific times when you'll unplug, such as during family meals or before bedtime, and stick to those boundaries.

Mindful Screen Time: Practice mindfulness when using technology. Be aware of how much time you spend on screens and consider whether it aligns with your priorities and responsibilities.

Quality Time: Prioritize quality time with family and loved ones over screen time. Engage in face-to-face conversations, play games, or participate in outdoor activities to foster meaningful connections.

Tech-Free Zones: Designate certain areas of your home as tech-free zones, such as the dinner table or the bedroom. These spaces should be reserved for non-digital interactions and relaxation.

Respect Family Rules: If you've established rules and guidelines for your children's tech use, make sure you follow them as well. Consistency reinforces the importance of these rules.

Digital Detox: Periodically engage in digital detoxes, where you intentionally disconnect from screens for a set period. This practice can help you recharge, reduce stress, and set a positive example.

Tech-Free Times: Create specific tech-free times during the day, such as the first hour after waking up and the last hour before bedtime. Use these times for self-care, reflection, or other non-digital activities.

Active Engagement: When using technology, be actively engaged in the content or activity. Avoid mindless scrolling or multitasking, which can lead to excessive screen time.

Online Etiquette: Model good online etiquette by using respectful language and tone in digital communications. Teach your children the importance of digital courtesy and empathy.

Privacy Awareness: Be mindful of your online privacy. Use strong and unique passwords, enable two-factor authentication, and avoid oversharing personal information on social media.

Critical Thinking: Encourage critical thinking skills by discussing online content with your children. Teach them how to evaluate the reliability of information and question what they encounter online.

Tech Education: Stay informed about the latest digital trends, apps, and platforms. This knowledge enables you to guide your children and make informed decisions about your own tech use.

Digital Well-Being: Prioritize your mental and emotional well-being. If you notice that certain online activities or platforms negatively impact your mood or mental health, consider limiting or avoiding them.

Respect Offline Time: When spending time with family and friends, respect their offline moments. Avoid excessive device use when in the company of loved ones to nurture meaningful relationships.

Continual Learning: Embrace continual learning about technology. Be open to exploring new digital tools, apps, and platforms, as this can expand your digital literacy and benefit your personal and professional life.

Responsible tech use by parents not only enhances their own digital well-being but also serves as a valuable model for their children. Children learn best by observing the behavior of trusted adults, so demonstrating balanced, respectful, and mindful tech use lays the foundation for responsible digital citizenship in the next generation.

Practical examples of responsible tech use by parents
Certainly, personal stories and insights can offer practical examples

of responsible tech use by parents. Here are a few anecdotes and insights:

Tech-Free Dinner Tradition: In our family, we've established a tech-free dinner tradition. During meals, we place our smartphones and other devices in a designated "phone basket." This practice encourages meaningful conversations and quality time together. My children have learned that dinner is a special time for connection, and they eagerly participate in this ritual.

Digital Detox Weekends: Once a month, we have "digital detox weekends" where our entire family disconnects from screens. We spend our time outdoors, playing board games, and exploring new hobbies. It's become an eagerly anticipated family bonding experience that helps us reset and appreciate the offline world.

Setting Time Limits Together: I involve my children in setting screen time limits. We discuss the importance of balancing tech use with other activities, such as homework, physical exercise, and reading. This collaborative approach empowers them to take ownership of their tech habits.

Online Etiquette Lessons: I've shared personal experiences of encountering both positive and negative online interactions with my children. We've discussed instances where kindness and empathy prevailed and cases where disrespectful behavior occurred. These discussions emphasize the importance of online etiquette and treating others with respect.

Privacy Awareness and Online Safety: I've used real-life examples to teach my children about online privacy and safety. We've discussed the potential risks of sharing personal information and the importance of safeguarding their digital footprint. These conversations have made them more vigilant and cautious online.

Balancing Work and Tech: As a working parent, I've had to find a balance between professional responsibilities and tech use. I've shared with my children how I manage my screen time during work hours and how I prioritize family time when I'm off-duty. This has helped them understand the importance of setting boundaries.

Admitting Mistakes: I've also been open about my own tech-related mistakes. For instance, I once fell into the trap of excessive social media scrolling, and I noticed it was affecting my mood. I shared this experience with my children to illustrate that even adults can make tech-related missteps, and it's okay to recognize and correct them.

Positive Tech Use: To promote positive tech use, I've encouraged my children to explore educational apps and creative projects online. We've engaged in collaborative digital activities, such as creating family photo albums or researching fun facts together. These experiences show them that technology can be a valuable tool for learning and creativity.

These personal stories and insights highlight how responsible tech use by parents can positively influence their children. By sharing experiences, setting boundaries, and actively engaging in both offline and online activities as a family, parents can instill important values and habits that contribute to responsible digital citizenship and overall well-being.

Technology as a Tool, not a Babysitter

The phrase "Technology as a Tool, Not a Babysitter" underscores an essential perspective on the role of technology in parenting and child development. It reminds us that while technology can offer educational and entertainment benefits, it should not replace essential parenting responsibilities or serve as a substitute for human interaction. Here's an exploration of this concept:

Quality Time vs. Digital Distraction: When parents rely too heavily on screens to occupy their children's time, it can lead to a lack of meaningful human interaction. Children need quality time with parents and caregivers to foster emotional bonds, develop social skills, and receive guidance and support.

Balancing Act: Technology can be a valuable tool when used mindfully. Educational apps, digital resources, and interactive media can enhance learning and creativity. However, parents should strike a balance between screen time and offline activities to ensure well-rounded development.

Learning Opportunities: Technology offers a plethora of educational opportunities. Parents can use it to supplement learning, explore new topics, and encourage curiosity. For instance, parents can engage in educational games or research projects together, leveraging technology as a resource for learning.

Teaching Tech Literacy: In today's digital age, tech literacy is an essential skill. Parents can teach their children how to use technology responsibly and safely. This includes understanding digital etiquette, recognizing online risks, and managing screen time effectively.

Supervision and Monitoring: Parents should play an active role in supervising and monitoring their children's tech use. This involves setting age-appropriate content restrictions, monitoring online interactions, and staying informed about the apps and websites their children are using.

Limiting Excessive Screen Time: Excessive screen time, especially passive consumption of media, can have adverse effects on children's physical and mental health. Parents should establish screen time limits based on age and ensure that their children engage in a variety of activities, including physical play and reading.

Modeling Responsible Use: Children learn by observing their parents' behavior. When parents model responsible tech use, including setting aside screens during family time, it reinforces the message that technology is a tool for specific purposes and not a constant distraction.

Communication and Connection: Technology should not hinder family communication and connection. Parents can encourage open dialogue about technology-related topics, including online safety, cyberbullying, and digital well-being. This fosters trust and ensures that children feel comfortable discussing their online experiences.

Creativity and Imagination: Parents can use technology to encourage creativity and imagination. Engaging in activities like digital storytelling, art projects, or coding together can harness the creative potential of technology.

Outdoor Play and Exploration: Outdoor play and physical activities are vital for children's physical development. Parents should ensure that technology does not replace time spent outdoors, exploring nature, and getting exercise.

"Technology as a Tool, Not a Babysitter" reminds parents to approach technology with intention and mindfulness. While technology can provide educational and entertainment value, it should complement, not replace, essential aspects of parenting, such as human connection, quality time, and well-rounded development. By striking a balance and using technology as a tool for specific purposes, parents can guide their children toward responsible and healthy tech use.

12

Staying Informed and Adapting

In the rapidly evolving digital landscape, staying informed and adapting to new technological developments is not only beneficial but also essential, especially for parents guiding their children through the digital age. Here's an exploration of the importance of staying informed and adapting:

Understanding the Digital World: Staying informed about the latest digital trends, platforms, and apps helps parents understand the digital world their children are growing up in. This knowledge enables parents to make informed decisions about their children's tech use and online activities.

Guiding Responsible Tech Use: The digital landscape is ever-changing, with new technologies and platforms constantly emerging. Parents who stay informed can guide their children in using these tools responsibly and safely, including recognizing potential risks and benefits.

Cybersecurity and Privacy: With the increasing prevalence of online threats and privacy concerns, parents must keep up-to-date with cybersecurity best practices and teach their children about online safety. This includes using strong passwords, recognizing phishing attempts, and protecting personal information.

Social Media and Trends: Social media platforms and trends can influence children's behavior and perceptions. Staying informed about the latest developments in social media allows parents to monitor their children's online interactions and address any concerns.

Parental Controls and Monitoring Tools: Technology offers various parental control and monitoring tools. Staying informed about these tools allows parents to choose the most appropriate ones for their family's needs and use them effectively.

Digital Literacy Education: As technology evolves, so do the skills required for digital literacy. Parents who stay informed can actively support their children's digital literacy education by teaching critical thinking, media literacy, and responsible online behavior.

Adaptability and Flexibility: Adaptability to new technologies and digital trends is a valuable skill for parents. It allows them to pivot and adjust their parenting strategies to address emerging challenges and opportunities.

Leading by Example: When parents stay informed and adapt to new technologies, they lead by example. Children learn the importance of continual learning and adaptability, crucial skills in the digital age.

Communication and Connection: Staying informed about the latest communication tools and platforms enables parents to connect with their children on the media they use. This facilitates open and ongoing communication about technology-related topics.

Empowerment and Confidence: Parents who are informed and adaptable feel more empowered and confident in navigating the digital landscape alongside their children. This confidence allows them to guide their children effectively and address any challenges.

11. Promoting Positive Tech Use: - Staying informed about positive and educational tech resources allows parents to actively encourage their children to use technology for creative and constructive purposes. This promotes a healthy relationship with technology.

12. Advocacy and Policy Awareness: - Well-informed Parents can advocate for policies and initiatives that promote online safety, digital literacy, and responsible tech use in their communities and schools.

In summary, staying informed and adapting to the ever-changing digital world is essential for parents as they navigate the challenges and opportunities of raising tech-savvy children. It enables parents to make informed decisions, guide responsible tech use, and foster a positive and safe digital environment for their families. Additionally, it sets an example of lifelong learning and adaptability, valuable qualities in the digital age.

Need for adapting rules and strategies as children grow

Adapting rules and strategies as children grow is essential for effective parenting and ensuring that your approach remains relevant to your child's changing developmental stages and needs. Here's why adapting is crucial:

Developmental Milestones: Children go through various developmental stages, each with its unique challenges and requirements. Adapting rules and strategies allows parents to address these milestones appropriately. For example, a toddler's needs differ significantly from a teenager's.

Increasing Independence: As children grow, they naturally seek more independence. Adapting rules and strategies allows parents to gradually grant more autonomy while still providing guidance and supervision when necessary.

Changing Interests: Children's interests evolve as they age. Adapting rules and strategies lets parents stay engaged with their children's interests and activities, fostering stronger bonds and effective communication.

Cognitive Development: As children's cognitive abilities develop, their capacity for understanding complex concepts and making informed decisions grows. Adapting rules allows parents to introduce more nuanced discussions about digital well-being, online safety, and responsible tech use.

Peer Influence: Peer influence becomes more significant as children grow older. Adapting strategies enables parents to address the impact of peer pressure and guide their children in making responsible choices, especially in the digital realm.

Technology Advances: Technology is constantly evolving. Adapting rules and strategies helps parents keep up with new platforms, apps, and digital trends. This knowledge is crucial for effectively monitoring and guiding children's tech use.

Emotional and Social Development: Adapting rules and strategies accommodates changes in emotional and social development. For instance, teenagers may require more privacy and autonomy in their digital interactions, while younger children may need closer supervision.

Responsible Decision-Making: Adapting rules and strategies allows parents to teach children responsible decision-making in various contexts, including online interactions, social media use, and digital etiquette.

Preparation for Adulthood: Adolescence is a critical time for preparing children for adulthood. Adapting strategies helps parents instill essential life skills, such as digital literacy, time management, and critical thinking, to equip their children for success in a tech-driven world.

Flexibility and Resilience: Adapting rules and strategies models flexibility and resilience to children. It teaches them the importance of adapting to changing circumstances and making informed choices as they encounter new challenges.

Healthy Parent-Child Relationships: Adapting rules and strategies with sensitivity to your child's growth fosters a healthy and supportive parent-child relationship. It shows that you respect their development and trust them to take on increasing responsibilities.

Individualized Parenting: Every child is unique. Adapting rules and strategies allows parents to tailor their approach to each child's personality, strengths, and weaknesses, ensuring that they receive the support and guidance they need.

In summary, adapting rules and strategies as children grow is a dynamic and responsive approach to parenting. It acknowledges the evolving needs, abilities, and interests of children and enables parents to provide effective guidance and support at every stage of their development. By adapting your parenting approach, you can foster healthy growth, digital literacy, and responsible tech use in your children while maintaining a strong and nurturing parent-child relationship.

Resources for staying updated on tech trends

Staying updated on tech trends is crucial for parents looking to guide their children in the digital age. Here are some resources to help you stay informed:

Tech News Websites: Websites like TechCrunch, CNET, Wired, Ars Technica, and The Verge provide in-depth coverage of the latest tech trends, gadgets, and industry developments.

Parenting Blogs and Websites: Parenting-focused websites often feature articles and guides on digital parenting and tech trends. Examples include Common Sense Media, Parenting.com, and Family Online Safety Institute (FOSI).

Online Forums and Communities: Platforms like Reddit have dedicated communities (subreddits) where tech enthusiasts discuss current trends, emerging technologies, and parenting-related tech issues. Subreddits like r/Parenting and r/technology can be valuable.

Social Media and Tech Influencers: Follow tech-savvy individuals and organizations on social media platforms like Twitter, Instagram, and YouTube. Tech influencers often share insights into the latest gadgets and tech trends.

Podcasts: Tech-related podcasts can be a convenient way to stay informed while multitasking. Shows like "Reply All," "The Vergecast," and "Note to Self" cover tech topics and digital culture.

YouTube Channels: YouTube hosts numerous tech channels that review gadgets, provide tutorials, and discuss emerging technologies. Channels like Marques Brownlee (MKBHD), Linus Tech Tips, and Unbox Therapy offer informative content.

Tech Magazines: Subscribe to Wired, PCMag, or MIT Technology Review for in-depth articles and features on the latest tech trends and innovations.

Online Courses and Webinars: Platforms like Coursera, edX, and LinkedIn Learning offer courses on tech-related topics. These courses can help you deepen your knowledge and stay updated.

Academic and Research Journals: Academic journals in fields like computer science and digital education often publish research on tech trends and their impact on children. Access to some academic journals may require a subscription.

Tech Conferences and Events: Attend tech conferences, webinars, and seminars. Events like CES (Consumer Electronics Show) and TED Talks often feature tech-related discussions.

Government and Nonprofit Organizations: Government agencies and nonprofit organizations focused on online safety and digital literacy, such as the Federal Trade Commission (FTC) and Common Sense Media, provide valuable resources and reports.

Parental Control Software Providers: Companies that offer parental control software often publish blogs and resources on digital parenting and tech trends. Explore resources from companies like Norton, Qustodio, and Bark.

Online Newsletters and RSS Feeds: Subscribe to newsletters from tech news websites or set up RSS feeds for tech-related topics to receive regular updates directly in your inbox or feed reader.

Educational Institutions: Universities and colleges may offer seminars, workshops, or online courses on digital literacy and emerging technologies. Check with local institutions for relevant opportunities.

Digital Well-Being Apps: Some apps and services, like Apple's Screen Time and Google's Digital Wellbeing, offer insights into your digital habits and can help you stay mindful of your tech use.

Technology Blogs and Vlogs: Many tech enthusiasts and experts maintain personal blogs or YouTube channels sharing insights and opinions on tech trends. These can provide a more personalized perspective.

Remember to verify the credibility of your information sources and seek diverse viewpoints to get a well-rounded understanding of tech trends. Staying informed is an ongoing process, but these resources can help you navigate the ever-evolving digital landscape effectively.

Parenting in the digital age can be both challenging and rewarding. Here's some encouragement and inspiration for parents as they navigate the complex landscape of raising tech-savvy, balanced children:

You're Not Alone: Remember that you're not the only parent facing the challenges of the digital age. Many parents share your concerns and are on a similar journey. Seek support and advice from online communities, parenting groups, and friends who can relate to your experiences.

Learning Together: Embrace the opportunity to learn and grow alongside your children. Technology is constantly evolving, and by staying curious and open to learning, you can model a lifelong learning mindset for your kids.

Small Steps Matter: Don't feel overwhelmed by the vastness of the digital world. Start with small, manageable steps to introduce technology to your children and set boundaries. Every positive interaction and conversation counts.

Communication is Key: Keep the lines of communication open with your children. Encourage them to share their online experiences, questions, and concerns. A trusting and supportive environment fosters healthy digital habits.

Be a Tech Role Model: Your tech habits and attitudes influence your children. By modeling responsible and balanced tech use, you're setting a powerful example for them to follow.

Adapt and Evolve: Parenting is a dynamic journey. Be prepared to adapt your rules and strategies as your children grow and as technology evolves. Flexibility is a key asset in parenting in the digital age.

Celebrate Offline Moments: Cherish and celebrate offline moments with your children. Engage in activities that don't involve screens, such as outdoor play, reading, arts and crafts, and family outings.

Focus on Quality Time: Quality time with your children is precious. Use technology as a tool to enhance your interactions, such as researching a shared interest or playing educational games together.

Empower Digital Literacy: Equip your children with the skills to navigate the digital world responsibly. Teach them how to think critically, evaluate online content, and practice good digital etiquette.

Safety First: Prioritize online safety and privacy. Educate your children about the potential risks of the internet and empower them with strategies to protect themselves.

Celebrate Achievements: Celebrate your children's achievements, both online and offline. Acknowledge their milestones, whether it's mastering a new tech skill or excelling in a non-digital hobby.

Stay Positive: While there are challenges in the digital age, there are also incredible opportunities for learning, creativity, and connection. Focus on the positive aspects of technology and harness them to enrich your family's life.

Seek Balance: Balance is key. Aim for a healthy equilibrium between screen time and offline activities. Remember that a balanced approach can lead to happier, more well-rounded children.

Trust Your Instincts: As a parent, you know your children best. Trust your instincts and make decisions that align with your family's values and needs.

Patience and Forgiveness: Parenting is a journey filled with ups and downs. Be patient with yourself and your children, and don't be too hard on yourself when things don't go as planned.

Unconditional Love: Above all, remember that your love and support are the most powerful tools in your parenting arsenal. Your children thrive when they know they are loved unconditionally.

You have the capacity to raise tech-savvy, balanced children who are prepared to navigate the digital world with confidence and responsibility. Your dedication, care, and commitment to their well-being will make a lasting impact on their lives. Embrace the journey, stay curious, and enjoy the moments you share with your children in this digital age.

About the Author

Isabella Trentwood is a visionary thinker and advocate for responsible digital citizenship among children. With a background in educational psychology and a personal journey through the triumphs and trials of parenting in the digital age, Isabella combines her professional expertise with real-world experience to guide families through the complexities of modern technology. Her passion for equipping parents with the tools to raise tech-savvy, balanced children shines through in her writing, workshops, and public speaking engagements.